KEY TO THE
MISSIONARY
PROBLEM

KEY TO THE MISSIONARY PROBLEM

Andrew Murray

Contemporized
by
Leona F. Choy

CHRISTIAN LITERATURE CRUSADE
Fort Washington. Pennsylvania 19034

CHRISTIAN LITERATURE CRUSADE
Fort Washington, Pennsylvania 19034

CANADA
Elgin, Ontario

GREAT BRITAIN
The Dean, Alresford, Hampshire

AUSTRALIA
P.O. Box 91, Pennant Hills, N.S.W. 2120

CONTENTS

PREFACE

The publisher and the contemporizer believe that it was not by chance but by God's sovereignty that this book was rediscovered during the research for the contemporary biography of Andrew Murray — exactly during the 150th anniversary of his birth in 1978. It had literally exploded on the Christian world when it was first issued and was used by the Lord to stimulate missionary zeal and action in many countries. Strangely, it dropped out of print until this volume.

Because Murray is best known for his devotional writings, it may seem incongruous to some that he addressed himself so strongly and knowledgeably to missions. But the connection will be understood upon reading the book. Does he speak relevantly or is his message dated and visionary, impractical for the multimedia, jet-impelled, sophisticated missionary enterprise of today? He dares to call his thoughts the "key" to the missionary problem. Is it a rusty key? Does it fit? The reader will be the judge.

Murray gives a hint of the timeless thrust of his book when he questions why, with millions of Christians in the world, the army of missionaries fighting the hosts of darkness is so small. His answer is — lack of heart. The enthusiasm of the kingdom is missing because there is so little enthusiasm for *the King*. Though much may be done by careful organization and strict discipline and good generalship to make the best of the few troops we

7

have, there is nothing that can so restore confidence and courage as the actual presence of a beloved King, to whom every heart beats warm in loyalty and devotion. "The missionary problem is a personal one."

By republishing this book in a contemporized form, we do not presume to supplant modern missionary strategies and principles of church growth, so academically and admirably arrived at. Rather, we offer it to provide a solid foundation for the missionary efforts of today. Without the proper launching pad, the rocket will fail to take off, abort, or in some other way fall short of the master intention. Without the underlying spiritual, Biblical, and personal principles which Murray sets forth as basic premises in this book, the missionary program of today and tomorrow will, to put it soberly, fizzle out like a wet firecracker instead of being the mighty missile that Christ intends and requires.

In this perspective, and prayerfully meditated upon, this book will keenly enrich missionary understanding. And it carries the thrust to catapult believers, in the power of the Holy Spirit, to successful involvement in every aspect of the Great Commission today.

1

Responses to the
Missionary Conference

It was my privilege to be invited to speak at the great Ecumenical* Missionary Conference held at New York in April, 1900. The circumstances of our country, South Africa, in which war had just broken out, were such that I did not feel at liberty to leave. An urgent letter from D.L. Moody, pressing me to come, and to stay over after the conference for the Northfield gatherings, reopened the question. But I was still kept from going.

The invitation, however, gave occasion to much thought and prayer. Did I have a message for that meeting? Would I be able to deliver that message so clearly as to make it worthwhile to go all that distance? Would it be possible amid the great variety of subjects, to secure quiet, time, and undivided attention for that which

*The term "ecumenical" as used by Murray and the New York Conference, in the context of that theological era, was intended in the positive biblical sense of inter-denominational. It was clearly an evangelical conference, not an inter-faith liberal gathering.

appeared to me the one thing needful?

In the midst of such questions, the thought that had long occupied my mind became clearer. I felt that the one point on which I would have wished to speak was this: How could the Church be aroused to know and to do our Lord's will for the salvation of men?

I had read with much interest the volume that had been issued in preparation for the Conference. I had received the impression that while very naturally the chief attention was directed to the work on the field, the work at the home base, in preparing the Church for doing its part faithfully, hardly had the place which its importance demands. There is no greater spiritual and mysterious truth than that Christ our head is actually and entirely dependent upon the members of His body for carrying out the plans which He, as Head, has formed. Only spiritual men, and a church in which spiritual men have influence, are capable of rightly carrying out Christ's commands. The clearest argument, the most forcible appeals, result in very little where this is not understood and aimed at as the true standard of Christian devotion. I feel very deeply that, to the friends of missions striving to see the whole perspective of the purpose of God and His kingdom, this is the most important question: How can we lead the whole Church to make herself available to the Lord for the work to which He has destined her and depends on her? In the preliminary report, the subject was hardly alluded to.

When I received the two volumes of the report of the conference, I naturally turned at once to see how far and in what way the question had been dealt with. I found many important suggestions as to how interest in missions may be increased. But, if I may venture to say, the root-evil, the real cause of so much lack of interest, and the way in which that problem could be met, was hardly dealt with. Indirectly it was admitted that there was something wrong with the greater part of professing Christians. But the real seriousness and sinfulness of the neglect of our Lord's command, indicated by a low state of Christian living, and the problem as to what the missionary organizations could do to change the situation, certainly did not take that prominent place which I think they deserve.

The following three headings will, I think, be found to cover all that was said in reference to the rousing of the Church to carry out her Lord's command.

The Pastor and the Pulpit

Of the suggestions made for putting missions in their proper place in the work of the Church, and in the heart of believers, the first dealt with *the Pastor and the Pulpit*. In an address on *The Pastor in Relation to the Foreign Field,* Dr. Pentecost opened with these words:

To the pastor belongs the privilege and the responsibility of solving the foreign missionary problem. Until the pastors of our churches wake up to the truth of this proposition, and the foreign work becomes a passion in their own hearts and consciences, our Boards may do what they can, by way of devising forward movements or organizing new methods for raising money from the churches, yet the chariot wheels of missions will drive heavily.

Every pastor holds his office under Christ's commission, and can only fulfill it when, as a missionary bishop, he counts the whole world his fold. The pastor of the smallest church has the power to make his influence felt around the world. No pastor is worthy of his office who does not put himself into sympathy with the magnificent breadth of the great commission, and draw inspiration and zeal from its worldwide sweep.

The pastor is not only the instructor, but the leader of his congregation. He must not only care for their souls, but direct their activities. If there are churches that do not give and do not pray for foreign missions, it is because they have pastors who are falling short of the command of Christ. I feel almost warranted in saying that, as no congregation can long resist the enthusiastic pastor, so, on the other hand, a congregation can hardly rise above cold indifference or lack of conviction regarding missions on the part of the pastor.

Dr. Cuthbert Hall spoke on *The Young Men of the Future Ministry and how to fire them with missionary passion:*

The passion of a Christ-like love for people develops in a Christian disciple from the presence in himself of powers and activities that reflect the mind of Christ. And what was the mind of Christ? A clear *vision* of what the world is and needs; a deep *feeling* of compassion towards the world; active *effort* for the world, even to giving His life a ransom for many. Out of this triad of powers issued the passion of His love of human lives — the boundless, fathomless, deathless love of Christ for man. The minister of Christ may speak with the tongues of men and of angels, may have all knowledge, may have a faith that could remove mountains, but *if he does not have the passion of a Christ-like love, he does not have the Spirit of Christ, and is none of His.*

The problem of the theological seminary is this: not how to train an occasional individual for the foreign field, *but how to kindle missionary passion in every person who passes through the school,* that he may thereby become an able minister of Christ. The essential thing is that there shall be within the school a sacred altar of missionary passion, at which the torch of every man shall be kindled, and the lip of every man shall be touched with the living coal. For the sake of those who possibly have gifts for service abroad, the theological seminary should be hot with zeal for evangelization, should be charged with solemn concern for the world's condition, so that not one could live within its walls without facing for himself the sober question, Is it Christ's will for me to go forth to serve Him in the regions beyond?

As for the man who shall enter the pastorate at home, he must have the missionary passion to make him great in understanding and apostolic in his view of Christ and Christianity. To overcome the resistance of ignorance and prejudice, to awaken the attention of apathetic minds blinded to the large question of the world's evangelization, to educate the Church's intelligence, to raise at home the supplies that shall maintain the work of God abroad, the pastor needs nothing less than missionary passion. *But the man who is thus to conquer must first himself be conquered and set on fire by God.*

The study of missions is slowly rising to the rank of a theological discipline. But the study of missions as a discipline of the theological seminary cannot by itself bring about a setting on fire of the future ministry with missionary passion. I see other forces at work which provide for that glorious end. I see developing a new concept of the ministry that is attracting many of the most gifted and consecrated of our young men. In many colleges today are found the very flower of our youth, to whom the ministry does not appear as a reserved and gloomy world of ecclesiastical technicalities, but as the king's own highway to joyful and abundant service. I see a spirit developing among our young people that is building up toward great missionary enthusiasm for the ministry of the future. Personal consecration for personal service is a concept of living that grows more and more attractive to many of our finest minds.

Out of this class of minds shall come the ministry of the future. It shall be a Christ-filled ministry, beholding the glory of God in the face of Jesus Christ, worshipping Him with the enthusiasm of an absolutely fearless affection, and presenting Him as the only Name under heaven whereby men can be saved. It shall be a missionary ministry, full of passion to redeem, clear-eyed to discover the ongoing of Christ's work, faithful in its stewardship at home and abroad; apostolic in its assurance that Christ has ordained it to bear much fruit, apostolic in its eagerness to spread far and wide the gospel of the risen and ascended Lord, apostolic in its hope that the unseen and crowned Saviour shall surely come again.

D. Brewer Eddy of the Yale Band gave the student viewpoint regarding pastors: "The importance of leadership must be emphasized. Let us use that talent which sets others to work. You are the leaders. We, six million young people in this land, are willing to follow you, if you will guide us. This is the responsibility of the pastor. The most definite impression, perhaps, of the

Yale Band is this: The praise or the responsibility and blame for present conditions in our missionary boards must be laid at the doors of the pastors. . . . If you base your appeal on grounds of pastor's pride, or of individual church benevolence, or of denominational loyalty, our young people will return a reward commensurate with the grounds from which such an appeal is made. But come to us with the deepest spiritual note you can sound, *with a message from the very life of the Master* we are learning to love more and more, and we six million will follow you to the best of our ability."

S. Earl Taylor continued to lay the responsibility on the pastors: "Until our pastors are ready to back this enterprise, there will never be a missionary spirit adequate to the needs of this generation. Where the pastor helps, almost any plan will succeed; where he is opposed, scarcely anything will succeed. While godly pastors in all parts of the country have been helping the students as they have worked in the churches, we are told here and in Great Britain that the greatest obstacle in arousing the home church is the pastor, who is afraid his salary will be cut down".

The Hon. S. B. Capen echoed the importance of leadership: "One condition is absolutely essential to success. While I believe we must expect our Christian laymen to have a large share in planning for this better organization, we shall still need devoted pastors to lead in its execution. The pastors are still to be the leaders in this mighty work, and a consecrated pastor will always mean a consecrated church. In this new epoch of missionary work the pastors of this generation, if they only will, may be the leaders in this holy war for righteousness in all the earth".

Rev. D. S. MacKay called attention to the pastor's work in depth: "A special appeal, to be effective, must have not only behind it, but in it, pulsating through it, the persuasive personality of the local pastor. To scatter a few leaflets in the pews, and simply call attention to them, is one of the surest ways by which a pastor can kill a special appeal. The effectiveness of the appeal depends, in the last instance, on the pastor who with loving zeal drives home the appeal. I do not deprecate in any way the helpfulness of missionaries from time to time in our pulpits, but it is the faithfulness of the local pastor, translating the special appeal into an individual message to his own people, that is, after all, the secret of success in foreign missions".

Will an emphasis on foreign missions detract from concern for the local church and community? On the contrary. Bishop Hendrix gave a concrete illustration: "Andrew Fuller, alarmed at the spiritual indifference of his church, preached a sermon on the duty of the Church to give the gospel to the world; and as he broadened their intellectual understanding, and stirred their zeal and their purpose, he followed it up the next Sunday with another sermon on the duty of the Church to give the gospel to the world. The third Sunday the same theme was presented from his pulpit. Then men began to inquire: 'If the gospel can save the world, can it also save our own children, our own community?' And from that *missionary* sermon sprang one of the most memorable revivals in the history of any church."

It is one thing for a minister to be an advocate and supporter of missions: it is another and very different thing for him to understand that missions are the chief end of the church, and therefore the chief end for which *his congregation* exists. It is only when this truth masters him in its spiritual power, that he will be able to give the subject of missions its true place in his ministry. He must see how every believer is called to witness to Christ's love and claim, and how healthy spiritual life depends on the share the believer takes in work for his Lord. He must learn how to lead the congregation on to make the extension of Christ's kingdom the highest object of its corporate existence.

In order to carry this out, the essential power lies in *a definite consecration to be filled with the Spirit and the love of Christ*. As he then thinks of all the ignorance and worldliness and unbelief that he has to contend with, he will learn that his missionary enthusiasm must not be of the flesh but the *enthusiasm of the Holy Spirit*. This will fill him with an intense love for Christ, an intense faith in His power, an intense desire to lead all His disciples to give their lives to make Jesus King over the whole earth.

The more earnestly we study missions in the light of the pastors' responsibility, the more we shall see that everything depends upon the personal life being wholly under the power of love for Christ, as the constraining power of our work. With the pastor, at least, it will be found that the missionary problem is a personal one.

The Pen and the Press

Next to the influence of the Pastor and the Pulpit in arousing interest in missions, the second place was given to the *Pen and the Press*. The need of preparing, circulating, and securing the study of mission literature was forcibly put from various points of view. The following paragraphs summarize the address.

Information is the fuel without which the fire cannot burn. Fuel is not fire, and cannot of itself create fire; but where there is fire, fuel is indispensable to keep it burning, or to make it burn with greater intensity. An informed Church will be a transformed Church. Possibly one of the greatest factors in the development of missionary interest is the systematic study of missions.

Missionary influence is twofold. The torch we hold up for others illuminates our own path. The Church is watching, and working, and praying for immortal souls. Our representatives are out in the thickest of the battle. It is a struggle between the forces of life and death. Are we so swathed in our small environment that we do not care for *news* of this contest with the forces of darkness? If we are in earnest to plant the Church of Christ in the ends of the earth, *let us hear the report of progress and pass it on.*

Ignorance is the source of weakness in missionary effort. *Know, and you will believe. Know, and you will pray. Know, and you will help in the front rank.*

A word on the demand that missionary publications should be interesting and attractive, like the so-called 'popular' magazines. What makes any publication popular? Why is it that during the recent campaigns in South Africa crowds of people jostled one another before the bulletin boards of the War Office? Unquestionably the intensity of the interest felt is *because of the issues involved,* affecting British prestige and power. *If Christians were as loyal to their King,* if they had the same eagerness for the establishment of His sovereignty over the regions which He claims, then messages from the battle line would be devoured eagerly! No tidings of this sort would be counted dull. Just here lies the difficulty in reference to missionary publications. *They will command the attention only of those who are at one with Christ in His world-wide redemptive work.* A church whose members, in fact as well as in profession, are seeking first the kingdom of God, will demand and will have fresh and full news of the progress of that kingdom throughout the earth. If once a quickened love for our Lord and His kingdom fills the hearts of His people, reports from the field of contest will be welcomed with eager acclaim.

Rev: Dr. Rankin reinforced the appeal: "When we have made our magazines as good as we can, what next? Then the pastors should tell the people about this literature. They should put it before them with such earnestness that they will feel that this is something they cannot afford to neglect. Our pastors should confer with the women of the churches, and let them take the magazines out among the people. Let our pastors glory in the mission literature. Let them feel that it is more important than everything else in telling the story of what is transpiring in the earth."

Dr. A. W. Halsey pointed the direction for our attitude: "It was said of the late Keith Falconer by one of his instructors, that he approached the world of ideas as great observers approach the world of nature, with wonder, with reverence, with humility. With such a spirit must the pastor approach the study of missionary literature. As you study the literature of missions, the conviction will deepen that though you are reading about the lives of Christians of many denominations and varied attainments, engaged in a great variety of work in different lands, yet the one fact that confronts you is that *these missionaries believe in the presence of the Spirit of God!* The pastor who neglects such literature robs his people of their birthright and wrongs his own soul. "

The People and the Pew

The third great means of awakening interest was that of *personal influence exercised through church related organizations*. There is great importance in having children, girls, boys, young people, men, women, all separately gathered under the influence of leaders who can expertly guide their training for the love and service of the kingdom. We must gratefully acknowledge the power teachers are already exercising, and must exercise still more largely, in receiving and passing on the wonderful love of Jesus Christ within the churches of the home lands, to train and prepare the future Church for giving herself to the work of missions.

Mrs. T. B. Hargrove made very plain the importance of workers with youth:

> The Church is truly thinking the thoughts of Christ after Him when she recognizes the importance of the child in the development of His kingdom on earth. Did not Jesus give children the chief place in the new dispensation, and affirm that the only way a man might understand God's truth was in getting back to his child-way of thinking? Truly, of children, and of men and women of child-like natures, is His kingdom here and hereafter to be made up.
>
> The young people's societies of the church are just like training schools where the workers of the future are being prepared to take the places of the veterans of today. Much time can be saved and greater efficiency secured if our youth un-interruptedly pursue the same methods of work, and labor for the same direct ends in their young

people's societies, that will engross their attention as missionary workers in the years to come.

A gentleman walking over a beautifully kept farm one day with his friend the owner, was admiring the skill and care everywhere manifested. He centered his attention upon the magnificent sheep, and with great earnestness asked how he had succeeded in rearing such flocks. The simple answer was, 'I take care of my lambs, sir.'

Did not the great Shepherd give His people the same rule? How shall we take care of the lambs? By keeping both juvenile and young people's societies under the care of *good shepherds.* They must have our very best; if a choice must be made for a superior leader between the adult's or the young people's work, *always give the young people the preference.* The crying need of the foreign missionary societies today, all over this broad land in every church, is for well-qualified teachers for juvenile and young people's societies. People are needed for this great task who love children and young people for their own sake, and for Christ's sake; persons of much experience, but young in heart; persons who feel themselves commissioned by Christ to 'feed My lambs'; persons who do not count time dear to themselves if by any means they may win souls for the Master. But these earnest intelligent workers need help. Adult members must look after the children and young people near and dear to themselves, and seek to lead them from juvenile to youth, and from youth to the adult societies. Oh! that the work of missions were really on all of our hearts! No weariness or toil would be spared, or self-denial counted, when our hearts are really enlisted.

Each youth worker should make it his first aim to inspire in every child real love for Christ and for the unevangelized. Perhaps the training of the young in their homes, in the schools and societies, is more defective just here than in any other one point.

Hearts truly won for Christ in the juvenile society, and tended lovingly and intelligently in the young people's society, will, in the great majority of cases, bring into our adult organizations Marys whose alabaster boxes of precious perfume will be broken at the Master's feet, and their fragrance reach to the uttermost parts of the earth.

The nineteenth century has brought especially to women many open doors, but none is of greater importance than this door: *The training of young minds and hearts in service for Christ, and for the world He died to redeem.* Let each realize that one of life's highest purposes is the development of the young people of our churches into noble Christian womanhood and manhood".

There is a great deal more of much value in connection with organization that took place at the Conference which I cannot refer to here. What I have quoted is enough to show how much will have to be done before the Church has fully availed herself of this wonderful power.

In summary, if our *pastors* are brought to believe that the great aim of the existence of their congregations is to make Christ known to every creature; if our people would read and take an interest in the *news of the kingdom and its extension;* if we could so get our Christian men and women of devotion to *organize our young people* so that their training in missionary service were part of their education in the love of Christ and the life of godliness; if our *students* could be trained in an atmosphere of missionary enthusiasm, there *would be* reason to hope that the work will be accomplished. Within thirty years every man and woman in the world would have the gospel brought within their reach, and actually offered to them.

Yet throughout all the addresses there is the secret admission that *in all these respects there is reason for anxiety.* Complaints were voiced about the lack of the missionary ideal and passion in many pastors and students, and the lack of interest by the majority of church members in missionary literature. Many, many more are needed to shepherd the young into the life of missionary devotion. These lacks prove that behind all these needs is a deeper need: *There is need of a great revival of spiritual life, of truly fervent devotion to our*

Lord Jesus, of entire consecration to His service. It is only in a church in which this spirit of revival has at least begun, that there is any hope of any very radical change in the relation of the majority of our Christian people to mission work.

I had hoped that this question, as the one of *paramount importance* in view of the possibility of carrying out Christ's command at once, would have absorbed the attention of the Conference. When the Student Volunteer Movement issued their appeal to the churches, announcing the motto they had adopted, *The Evangelization of the World in this Generation*, their message met with a most enthusiastic welcome and response. Must we now wait for them to come a second time, and ask the Church what the great hindrance is that holds Christ's people back from meeting the emergency with the enthusiasm which He has a right to claim? It is time that some representative body appeal to all fellow-Christians, and call for an inquiry into the nature and extent of the disease that is so paralyzing the Church. At the same time we need to know the conditions for restoration to health and strength. To know what is wrong, and with confession and humility to turn from it to the loving Lord, would bring new life to the Church, and *altogether new power for the work that has to be done*.

It is under the spiritual burden of such thoughts that I felt led to write this book. I know that it is no easy task to speak humbly, wisely, lovingly, and yet faithfully and effectually, of what appears lacking or sinful in the

Church. And yet I am sure that there are many who would welcome help in answering the questions: Is there any real possibility of such a revival in the Church that in every congregation where the full gospel is preached, her most important aim will be to carry the gospel to every creature? What is the path that will lead to this change? And what steps should be taken by those who lead the missions of the Church?

May God by His Holy Spirit guide us to the vision of His will concerning His Church, to the faith in His power and promise, and to the obedience that will walk in any path He opens up.

2

Missions: A Test of the State of the Church

In the previous chapter, I raised the question, What can be done to so stimulate the spiritual life of the Church that the missionary cause shall have all the hearty enthusiasm and support which it deserves? To answer that question we must first form an accurate appraisal of the real relationship of the Church to mission work.

In this chapter we will consider the state of the Church. As the basis of our study, we will take passages from addresses given at the Conference. The frequent use of the word IF points out to us how the Church has failed in her duty, and suggests the state in which she should and could be found. Moreover, we must ask the cause of failure, and what cure might be found for such a condition.

Notice Dr. John R. Mott's emphasis from the following:

The Moravians have done more in proportion to their ability than any other body of Christians. *IF members of Protestant Churches in Great Britain and America gave in like proportion,* missionary contributions would aggregate a fourfold increase. *IF we went out as missionaries in corresponding numbers,* we would have a force of nearly 400,000 foreign workers, which is vastly more than the number of missionaries estimated as necessary to achieve the evangelization of the world in this generation. I ask the question, *What has there been in connection with their work which is not reproducible?*

The world-wide proclamation of the gospel can be accomplished by this generation, *IF it has the obedience and determination* to attempt the task. There is not a single country on the face of the earth to which the Church, *IF she seriously desired,* in our time, could not send ambassadors of Christ to proclaim His message.

Contrast the millions of members in Protestant Churches with the few thousand which on the day of Pentecost began the work. As we recall the achievements of that infant Church, can we deny the possibility of present day Christians to give all mankind an opportunity to know Christ, *IF they united to accomplish it.*

The money-power of the Church is enormous. *IF only one-fourth of the members* of Protestant churches gave one cent a day, it would yield over twenty-five million pounds, in contrast with the less than four million pounds of the past year.

The various Christian young people's organizations include, in North America alone, fully six million members. These young people themselves, *IF properly educated and guided,* are able to raise each year enough money to support all the foreign missionaries to accomplish the evangelization of the world.

Sunday schools contain over twenty million members. *IF these were trained* to give a penny per week, it would yield an amount greater than the present total missionary gifts of Christendom.

There are now probably two hundred thousand soldiers at the Cape (South Africa). We have all been impressed by the exhibition of the unity and power of the British Empire; we have been deeply moved by the example of the republics, as we have seen old men and boys going out to fight the battles of their country; and yet, when it is suggested that all Protestant Christendom unite in sending out fifty thousand missionaries the thought is criticized as being visionary *and placing too severe a strain on the resources of the Church!*

The Bible Societies are more than eighty in number. *IF the work is properly promoted,* before this generation closes, each person in Asia and Africa will be able to read or hear in his own language the wonderful works of God.

Bishop Thoburn said that *IF this Conference and those whom it represents will do their duty,* within the first decade of the new century ten million people can be gathered into the Church of Christ. Dr. Chamberlain affirmed the possibility of bringing India under the sway of Christ within the lifetime of some, at least, in this assembly!

In his address, Mr. Robert Speer similarly declared: "The aim of foreign missions is to make Jesus Christ known to the world. The Church could do the work, *IF this aim ruled her spirit.* I was glad to read, on the first page of our program, those dying words of Simeon Calhoun: 'It is my deep conviction, and I say it again and again, that *IF the Church of Christ were what she ought to be,* before twenty years would pass the story of the Cross would be proclaimed in the ears of every living man.' "

And—to quote only one more instance—Rev. W. Perkins, Secretary of the Wesleyan Missionary Society, London, said: "Great as are the results of foreign missions, over which we rejoice and give thanks, they would have been a hundredfold greater, *IF the Church had been what she ought to be in the two great matters of prayer and giving.*"

The foregoing IFS all indicate something wrong in the Church in reference to Christ's command to evangelize the world. We all know the force of the word IF. It suggests a cause from which certain effects can follow. It points to the condition needed to ensure the results we desire. In the passages we have quoted, and in different forms of expression frequently recurring in missionary literature, we find the same thought incessantly repeated: How certainly and speedily the evangelization of the world could be accomplished if it were not for the failure of the Church in doing the part that has been assigned her by God.

Such statements are not important in themselves. More important are the lessons we ought to learn, and what can be done to roll away the reproach resting on us as a Church of Christ. These IFS suggest four questions: Is the Church really at fault, and how? Is it possible for her to have actually done what was claimed? What is the cause of the present failure? How is deliverance from this evil to be found?

These charges against the Church were not brought by unbelievers or enemies, but by some of the Church's most faithful servants. They were spoken in the presence of thousands of missionaries and mission friends. If they were not true they would have been denied and refuted. But no one could deny them. However devotedly a small part of the Church is doing its utmost, the great majority of her members are not what they should be. *They do not truly desire* to make Christ known to every creature as speedily as possible. *This aim does not rule the spirit of the Church — she is not prepared to do her duty.*

The charge is extremely serious and solemn. It is not good enough just to listen and then lay it aside and forget it. Everyone who loves Christ's Church, who loves Christ Jesus his Lord, who loves the souls that are perishing through this neglect, ought to pause and consider what it means. Christ has given His life in serving us, and asked us to give our lives in serving Him; Christ has put His dying love into our hearts, and asked us to impart it to others; Christ in His love has died for all, and has made Himself dependent on us to let them know of that love; Christ has endured the agony of the cross for the joy of winning and saving the perishing, and has counted on our love to delight in making Him happy and bringing Him His reward.

Yet the great majority of those who profess to owe everything to His dying love, are utterly indifferent either as to pleasing Him or blessing their fellowmen by winning them to that love. Surely His love can never have been a reality to them, or they could not so neglect their calling. Can it be that they have never been correctly taught what they have been redeemed for? The Church, in calling them to seek salvation for themselves, must have kept hidden from them the great purpose for which they were redeemed — that they should live to save others. Whatever be the cause, here is the solemn fact — a Church, purchased by the blood of the Son of God to be His messenger to a dying world, *for the greater part has failed entirely to understand and fulfill her calling.* No words can express, no mind can grasp, the terrible meaning and consequences of the failure and condemnation involved in the simple IFS of which we speak.

And let us not think that this failure is because of some natural impossibility. These IFS point to *what is the Church's actual destiny.* Dreamers speak of impossibilities, and calculate what might be done if they came true. We are listening to men who are speaking words of soberness and truth. These IFS suggest *what is certainly and divinely possible.* They point us to the Church of Pentecost.

"To evangelize the world in this generation is possible," they say, "in view of the achievements of the Christians of the first generation. They did more to accomplish the work than has any succeeding generation. In studying the secret of what they accomplished, one is led to the conclusion that they employed no vitally important method which cannot be used today, and that they availed themselves of no power which we cannot utilize."

The mighty power of God and His Holy Spirit are ours as well as theirs. We are heirs to all that the Church of Pentecost had: The power of His dying love in the heart; a triumphant faith in Christ; simple, bold, personal testimony; patient suffering; absolute passionate consecration; the heavenly power that overcomes the world and makes us more than conquerors through Him that loved us.

As was pointed out, the Moravian Church was one of the smallest in number and poorest in means of all the churches. What it has done is a proof that the whole Church, when once she rouses herself to her calling, *most surely can accomplish the work.* In view of the opportunities which the Church has in the open doors in every country of the world, of the enormous resources the

Church possesses in the wealth of her members, in the numbers of workers over which the Church has disposal, and the faith that to send them out would, instead of weakening it, bring quickening and strength, *it is absolutely within the power of the Church to bring the gospel to every creature within this generation.* Let us take time to come under the full power of this great thought. It will give force to what has been said about the terrible failure of the Church. It will prepare us for discovering how to deal with the evil.

These IFS *invite us to ask* the causes of this shortcoming. Why has the Church of Christ been so utterly unfaithful? Does not our Protestant Christendom profess, and that honestly, to acknowledge Christ as its Lord, and God's holy Word as the law of its life? Is it not our boast that we are in the true succession of the Pentecostal Church, the heirs of all her promises and powers? Are we not the children of the Reformation, in possession of the great truths that every man has a right to God's Word as taught him by God's Spirit, and a free access through Christ to God's pardoning grace? And is it not the very sum and center of our profession, that we acknowledge Jesus as Master and Lord, and have given ourselves to do what He says? Then why is it that, in the very thing on which Christ's glory most depends, on which His heart of love is most set, the Church should have failed to realize or fulfill her destiny?

It would be easy to mention many causes that co-operate in producing this unfaithfulness. But they may all be summed up in one answer: *The low spiritual state of the Church as a whole.* The control of the Holy Spirit in power and fulness over the life of believers is essential to the health and strength of the Church. Scripture teaches us how easy it is for a Church and its members to have a sound creed, a faithful observance of services and duties, a zeal for the extension of the Church and for works of philanthropy which are within the range of human nature, while that which is definitely spiritual, supernatural, and divine is to a large extent lacking. The spirit of the world, the wisdom and the will of man in the teaching of the Word and the guidance of the Church, make it very much like any other human institution. There is little of the power of the heavenly world and eternal life to be seen in her. In such a Church missions may still have a place, though not the place nor the power which is needed for fulfilling the command of Christ. The passion of love to Christ and to souls, the enthusiasm of sacrifice for men, and of faith in the omnipotent Power that can quicken the dead, is lacking.

Among the chief symptoms of this sickly state are *worldliness and lack of prayer.* If there is one thing that Christ and Scripture insist on, it is that His kingdom is not of this world, that the spirit of the world cannot understand the things of God; that separation from the world in fellowship and conduct, in surrender to the Spirit who is from heaven, is essential to the faithful following of the Lord Jesus. The one universally admitted fact — that the majority of Christians care nothing and give nothing for missions, that a large number give but little and not from the highest motives, is simply a proof of the worldliness in which most Christians live. It needed Christ to come from heaven to save men out of the world. It needs the Spirit of heaven in Christ's disciples to free them from the spirit of the world, to make them willing to sacrifice all to win the world for Christ. *It needs the same Spirit, through whom Christ gave His life for the world, to revive His Church to win the world for God.*

Lack of prayer is another symptom of this sickly state. A wordly spirit in the Christian hinders his praying. He looks at things in the light of the world. He is not at home in heavenly places. He does not realize the dark power of sin in those around him, or the urgent need of direct divine intervention. He has little faith in the efficacy of prayer, in the need of much and unceasing prayer, in the power there is in him to pray in Christ's name and prevail. True charity, the giving from devotion to Christ and for Him, and true prayer, the asking and counting upon Him to bless the gift and bestow His Spirit in His work, are proof that the worldly spirit is being overcome, and that the soul is being restored to spiritual health. IF the Church is to be what she ought to be, and to do what her Lord asks her to do for the evangelization of the world, this sickness and failure must be acknowledged, and deliverance sought.

These IFS urge us to ask *how such deliverance can be found.* What is the cure for this diseased state? A sickly man cannot do a healthy man's work. To help carry Christ's cross to the world needs the vigor of full spiritual health. How can we find this?

The *first step* in returning to God for true service and new blessing, *is always confession.* The leaders of the Church's mission work, who ought to know the tremendous needs of the world, who understand the meaning and urgency of our Lord's command, who feel the utterly inadequate provision the Church is making for His work — on them rests the solemn duty of lifting up their voices and making God's people know their sin. It is possible that we are all so occupied with our special fields of labor, and the thought of how much is being done, that the extent and guilt of what is not being done is comparatively lost sight of.

The latest statistics tell us that, at the close of the 19th century, the total of communicants from among the unevangelized as the fruit of mission work was 1,300,000. The Christian community in unevangelized lands or the number of people in nominal adherence to Christianity and within direct touch of gospel agencies, is 4,400,000 (Dr. Dennis in the Report of the Conference, Vol. 2. p. 423). With a thousand million unevangelized, we are thus in real contact with less than five million as against 995 million still unreached! Until Christians are led to listen, and think, and pray for opened eyes to look upon these fields, "white unto the harvest," entrusted to them, they never will recognize the greatness of the work, their own unpreparedness, or the urgent need of *waiting for divine power to fit them for the task.*

As we take this in, we shall feel and confess how little the Church has done. The guilt and shame resting on body of Christ will become the Lord's burden on us. We rejoice and give thanks for the 15,460 foreign missionaries who are now in the field laboring among the four million in Christian communities of their lands. But what efforts are being made to reach the one thousand million? They are dying at the rate of over thirty million a year — within thirty years they will have passed away into the darkness. What prospect is there that they will be speedily reached?

Every mission organization complains of lack of funds. We are told that of church members one-third neither gives nor cares for the kingdom; that another third gives but cares very little, and does not give from the right motive; and that even of the remaining third — it is really less than a third — only a small proportion are doing their utmost, and giving and praying with their whole heart. The disobedience of the Church in the great majority of her members, her neglect of her Lord's work, her refusal to listen to the appeals to come to His help — is not this a sin and a guilt greater than we think? If the Church is really to awaken out of her sleep, the one thing needed is that those to whom God has given the charge of His mission work in the world, should lay before the people the *the utter disproportion between what is being done, and what ought to be and can be done.* They should press home the guilt and the shame of it until an increasing number bow before God in confession and humility and with a cry for pardon and mercy as earnest as when they sought their own salvation.

With the appeal to men there must be the appeal to God. The work is His: He cares for it. The power is His: He gives it. The Church is His: He waits to use it. The world is His: He loves it. He can make His people willing in the day of His power. He will hear the cries of His servants who give Him no rest. He delights to prove His faithfulness in fulfilling His promises. *Things cannot go on as they are if the world is really to be evangelized in this generation.* In this generation every person must have the gospel offered to him. Unless there is a great change in the Church, *and she give herself to the work in a way she has not yet done,* the work cannot be accomplished. But it can, if God's people will fall upon their faces before Him to confess their sin and the sin of their breathren.

Let them ask God to reveal the cause of all the failure, and then take the message to His Church. Let them preach the great truth, that as the winning of the world to God is the supreme purpose of the Church's existence, so the love of souls, the surrender of the whole life to Christ for His use in the winning of souls, is the duty, is the only healthy life, for every believer. There are tens of thousands of God's children who are willing, yes, who are secretly longing, to serve their Lord, but don't know how, or don't have the courage to do so.

Then the time will come when we shall no longer have to say, *"IF the Church were what she ought to be",* but shall find our joy and strength in guiding a prepared people in that arduous but blessed path of bearing Christ's cross to every man on God's earth, and wrestling with the hosts of hell to make way for the kingdom of Christ the conqueror!

3

Love to Christ
as Motivation

At the turn of the century, Dr. John R. Mott declared: "The most striking example of achievement on the home field, in the interest of foreign missions, is that of the Moravians. They have done more, in proportion to their numbers, than any other body of Christians. *IF members of Protestant Churches in Great Britain and America gave in like proportion,* the missionary contributions would aggregate a fourfold increase. And *IF they went out as* missionaries in corresponding numbers, we would have a force of nearly 400,000 foreign workers, which is vastly more than the number of missionaries estimated as necessary to achieve the evangelization of the world. The question is, What is there in connection with their work which we are not reproducing?"

In the Conference, the Secretary of the Board of Missions of the Moravian Church in the United States,

Rev. P. de Schweinitz, summed up the work of the Church in these words—

"Even to-day (in 1900) the Moravians have for every fifty-eight communicants in the home churches a missionary in the foreign field, and for every member in the home churches there are more than two members in the congregations where their missionaries labor. What was the incentive for foreign missionary work which has produced such results? While acknowledging the supreme authority of the Great Commission, the Moravian Brethren have always emphasized as their chief incentive the inspiring truth from Isaiah 53:10-12: making our Lord's suffering the spur to all their activity. From that prophecy they drew their missionary battle-cry: *'To win for the Lamb that was slain, the reward of His sufferings.'* We feel that we must compensate Him in some way for the awful sufferings which He endured in working out our salvation. The only way we can reward Him is by bringing souls to Him. That is compensation for the travail of His soul. In no other way can we so effectively bring the suffering Saviour the reward of His passion as by missionary labor, whether we go ourselves or enable others to go. Get this burning thought of 'personal love for the Saviour who redeemed me' into the hearts of all Christians, and you have the most powerful incentive for missionary effort. Oh! if we could make this missionary problem a personal one! If we could fill the hearts of the people with a personal love for this Saviour who died for them, the indifference of Christendom would disappear, and the kingdom of Christ would appear."

If the example of the Moravian Brethren is to exercise any influence, and the Church to be aroused to follow in their footsteps, we must find out what the principles were that animated them, where they got the power that enabled them to do so much, and especially, how God fitted them for doing that work. We cannot have like effects without like causes. As the conditions of their successes are discovered, the path to restoration for the Church today can be found.

A short summary of the history of the Moravian Church will be found full of helpful instruction.

Its Origin: Moravia and Bohemia were two provinces in the north-west of the Austrian Empire, bordering on Saxony.* In the seventh and eighth centuries they received the knowledge of the gospel first from the Greek, later from the Roman Church. As the former allowed preaching in the national language, and gave them the Bible in their own language, there arose divisions which were the cause of unceasing conflict. Gradually the Roman Church got the upper hand, and from the beginning of the fifteenth century, when John Huss was burned at the stake for preaching the gospel (1415), the country was the scene of terrible persecutions. In course of time those who remained faithful to the gospel gathered in a village in the north-east of Bohemia, in the valley of Kunwald, where they were allowed for a time to live in comparative peace. Here, in 1457, they were

---

*Geographical designations are stated as they existed at the time of writing.

known as "The Brethren of the Law of Christ." When their Church was established, they assumed the name of *The United Brethren.*

Its Discipline: One of the brightest jewels of this church was its discipline. It was not only their doctrine, but their life; not only their theory, but their practice, that gave them such power. When the Reformers became acquainted with them later, Bucer wrote, "You alone, in all the world, combine a wholesome discipline with a pure faith. When we compare our Church with yours, we must be ashamed. God preserve to you that which He has given you."

Calvin wrote, "I congratulate your churches that the Lord, in addition to pure doctrine, has given them so many excellent gifts, and that they maintain such good morals, order, and discipline. We have long since recognized the value of such a system, but cannot in any way attain to it."

And Luther said, "Tell the brethren that they should hold fast that which God has given them, and not relinquish their constitution and discipline."

And what was their discipline? In every detail of their lives — in business, in pleasure, in Christian service, in civil duties — they took the Sermon on the Mount as a lamp to their feet. They counted the service of God the one thing to live for, and everything was made subservient to this. Their ministers and elders were to keep watch over the flock, to see that all were living to the glory of God. All were to be one brotherhood, helping and encouraging one another in a quiet and godly life.

Its Sufferings: For some 50 years they lived in Kunwald relatively unmolested, though persecuted elsewhere. At the turn of the century, the Pope and the King combined against them. In 1515, just as the Reformation was dawning in Germany, it almost looked as if they would be extinguished. With intervals of toleration, their troubles continued, until in 1548 a Royal Edict drove thousands to Poland, where they established a large and prosperous Church. With a new King in 1556 peace returned, and the Brethren's Church was again firmly established, and divided into the three provinces of Bohemia, Moravia, and Poland. By the end of the century the Church had given a Bible to the people, and had fostered education to such a degree that the Bohemian schools had a noted reputation in Europe, the people being considered the best educated people in the world. In 1609 they obtained the Bohemian Charter, for the first time giving full religious liberty. In 1616 they published their *Order of Discipline,* with a full account of the institution of the church.

Its Suppression: With the accession of Frederick II, everything suddenly changed. The Day of Blood at Prague, in 1620, witnessed the execution of 27 of the leading nobles. During the six years that followed, Bohemia was a field of blood, and 36,000 families left the country. The population dwindled from 3,000,000 to 1,000,000. The Church of the Brethren was broken up and scattered. During the whole century those who stayed in the country worshipped God in secret, and formed what was called, "The Hidden Seed." When we take up the thread again, in 1722, just a hundred years will have elapsed, during which only God knows what was suffered. Yet even during that period hope was not altogether dead. John Amos Comenius, the last bishop of the Church in Moravia, wrote in 1660: "Experience clearly teaches that particular churches are sometimes destroyed by the hand of God stretched out in wrath. Yet sometimes other churches are either planted in their stead, or the *same churches rise in other places*. Whether God will deem her worthy to be revived in her native land, or let her die there, and resuscitate her elsewhere, we know not . . . According to His own promise, the gospel will be brought, by those Christians who have been justly chastened, to the remaining peoples of the earth; and thus, as of old, our fall will be the riches of the world."

In 1707 similar words were spoken by George Jaeschke, one of the few witnesses to the truth at that time. He was the father of Michael Jaeschke, and grandfather of Augustin and Jakob Neisser, who with their wives and children formed the first party led to Herrnhut. On his deathbed, at the age of eighty-three, he spoke: "It may seem as though the final end of the Brethren's Church has come. But, my beloved children, you will see a great deliverance. The remnant will be saved. I do not know whether this deliverance will come to pass here in Moravia, or whether you will have to go out of 'Babylon'; but I do know it will transpire not very long hence. I am inclined to believe that an exodus will take place, and that a refuge will be offered on a spot where you will be able, without fear, to serve the Lord according to His holy word."

A Place of Refuge: The Lord had indeed provided for His people a place of refuge, where the Church of the Brethren would be renewed. It was in 1722 that Christian David received from Count Nicholas Louis Von Zinzendorf permission to bring refugees from Moravia to his estate in Saxony. Christian David had been born a Roman Catholic, but could find no rest in his church. As a soldier in Saxony he found Christ from the teaching of a godly Lutheran pastor. He returned to Moravia to preach the Saviour he had found, and spoke with such power that an awakening followed. Persecution was immediately aroused, and the preacher went to find a refuge for the persecuted. When he had obtained Zinzendorf's permission, he returned and led out his first band of ten, who reached Berthelsdorf in June 1722. Time after time this devoted servant of the Lord went back to preach the gospel, and to lead out those who were willing to forsake all. In this way it was not long before some 200 had gathered, many of them among those who had been called "The Hidden Seed," the true descendants of the old Brethren. The spot allotted to them had been called Hutberg — the Watch Hill. They called their new settlement Herrnhut — the Lord's Watch. They took the word in its double meaning: The Watch of the Lord *over them;* the Watch of the Lord to be kept *by them* in prayer and waiting for His leading, which was to be their safety.

The New Leader: Such was the material God had gathered at Herrnhut to build a house for Himself. Let us turn for a moment to the man whom He had prepared, as a wise master-builder, to superintend the work. Count Zinzendorf was born in May 1700, of godly parents. On his dying bed his father had taken the child, then only six weeks old, in his arms, and consecrated him to the service of Christ. "Already in my childhood," wrote Zinzendorf, "I loved the Saviour, and had abundant communion with Him. In my fourth year I began to seek God earnestly, and determined to become a true servant of Jesus Christ."

At Franke's school in Halle, at the age of twelve, he often met missionaries, and his heart was touched with the thought of work for Christ among the unevangelized. Among the boys at school he founded the "Order of the Mustard Seed." They bound themselves to be kind to all men, to seek their welfare, and to try to lead them to God and to Christ. As an emblem they had a small shield, with an *Ecce Homo,* and the motto, "His wounds our healing." Each member wore a ring, on which was inscribed, "No man liveth unto himself." Before leaving Halle he entered into a covenant with an intimate friend for the conversion of the unevangelized, especially such as would not be cared for by others. From Halle he went to Wittenberg, where he held prayer-meetings for the other students, and often spent whole nights in prayer and study of the Bible.

It was about this time that Zinzendorf visited the picture gallery in Dusseldorf, where he saw the *Ecce Homo* painting by Sternberg, with the words underneath:

"All this I did for thee,
What hast thou done for Me?"

His heart was touched. He felt as if he could not answer that question. He turned away more determined than ever to spend his life in the service of his Lord. The vision of that face never left him. Christ's love became the constraining power of his life. "I have," he exclaimed, "but one passion — 'tis He, and He only." It was His dying love that fitted Christ for the work God had given Him as the Saviour of men. It was the dying love of Christ mastering his life that fitted Zinzendorf for the work he had to do.

The Revival of the Church: When Zinzendorf settled on his estate, he devoted himself to the spiritual welfare of his tenants. With three like-minded friends he formed the "League of the Four Brethren." The object was to proclaim to the world the "universal religion of the Saviour and His family of disciples, the heart-religion in which the Saviour is the central point." He joined the pastor of the congregation in preaching, in meetings for prayer and singing. He lived for Christ and the souls He had died to save.

In offering the Moravian exiles a refuge on his estate, he had simply thought of giving them a home, in which, as his tenants, they should earn their livelihood and be free in the exercise of their religion. When it was known that Herrnhut was a refuge for the persecuted, all sorts of religious displaced persons came to seek a home there.

The Spirit of discord speedily entered, and there was danger of its becoming a seat of sectarianism and fanaticism. Zinzendorf felt that the time had come for him to intervene. He had faith in the uprightness and earnestness of the Moravian settlers. He gave himself personally to loving dealings with the leaders.

Many of them had felt deeply the sin and pain of division, and had been praying that, by the grace of God, the spirit of true fellowship might be restored. With many tears and prayers, in the love and patience of Jesus Christ, the Count pleaded with those who were in error. One point on which the Moravian Brethren (they were more than 200 out of the 300) would not give way was their unwillingness to be absorbed into the Lutheran Church. They insisted on having the discipline of the old Moravian Church maintained. The Count was afraid that this might give rise to prejudice and misunderstanding in the church around them, but he felt that their claim was just, and resolved at any risk to yield to them. The principles and discipline of the old Moravian Church were to be restored. Zinzendorf drew up the Statutes, Injunctions and Prohibitions, according to which they were to live.

On May 12, 1727 (just five years after the first arrivals), a memorable day in the history of the Brethren, he called them all together and read to them the "statutes" that had been agreed on. There was to be no more discord. Brotherly love and unity in Christ were to be the golden chains that bound them together. All the members shook hands and pledged themselves to obey the Statutes. That day was the beginning of new life in Herrnhut.

It was recorded: "This day the Count made a covenant with the Lord. The Brethren all promised, one by one, that they would be the Saviour's true followers. Self-will, self-love, disobedience — they bade these farewell. They would seek to be poor in spirit; no one was to seek his own profit before that of others; everyone would give himself to be taught by the Holy Spirit. By the mighty working of God's grace all were not only convinced but, as it were, carried along and mastered."

On the 12th of May 1748 the Count wrote: "Today, twenty-one years ago, the fate of Herrnhut hung in the balance, whether it was to become a sect, or to take its place in the Church of our Saviour. After an address of three or four hours, the power of the Holy Spirit decided for the latter. The foundation principle was laid down, that we were to set aside the thought of being Reformers, and to look after ourselves. What the Saviour did after that, up to the winter, cannot be expressed. The whole place was indeed a veritable dwelling of God with men; and on the 13th of August it passed into continual praise. It then quieted down, and entered the Sabbath rest."

The 12th of May has been called the birthday of what was henceforth known as *The Renewed Church;* the 13th of August was its baptism with the Holy Spirit. After the Statutes had been adopted, and all had bound themselves to a life of obedience and love, the spirit of fellowship and prayer was greatly increased. Misunderstandings, prejudices, secret estrangements were confessed and put away. Prayer was often in such power that those who had only given external assent were convicted, and either changed or inwardly felt compelled to leave.

The Count had had to leave home for a time, and on his return, the 4th of August, brought with him a copy of the *History of the Moravian Brethren,* that he had found which gave the full account of the ancient discipline and order. This caused great joy. It was taken as a token that the God of their fathers was with them. As one of them wrote: "Under the cloud of our fathers we were baptized with their spirit; signs and wonders were seen among us, and there was great grace on the whole neighborhood." The whole next night was spent by the Count and the Brethren in prayer, with a great gathering in the hall at midnight. The following days all were conscious in the singing-meetings of a strange overwhelming Power. On Sunday, the 10th, Pastor Rothe was leading the afternoon meeting at Herrnhut, when he was overpowered and fell on his face before God. The whole congregation bowed under the sense of God's presence, and continued in prayer till midnight. He invited the congregation to the Holy Supper on the next Wednesday.

As it was the first communion since the new fellowship, it was resolved to be specially strict and to make use of it "to lead the souls deeper into the death of Christ, into which they had been baptized." The leaders visited *every member,* seeking in great love to lead them to true heart-searching. In the evening of Tuesday, at the preparation service, several passed from death to life, and the whole community was deeply touched.

On that Wednesday morning all went to Berthelsdorf. On the way there, those who had felt estranged from another bound themselves together afresh. During the singing of the first hymn a wicked man was powerfully convicted. The presentation of the new communicants touched every heart, and while the hymn was being sung it could hardly be recognized whether there was more singing or weeping. Several brethren prayed, especially pleading that, since they were exiles out of the house of bondage, they did not know what to do, and they desired to be kept free from separation and sectarianism; they besought the Lord to reveal to them the true nature of His Church, so that they might walk unspotted before Him, and might not abide alone but be made fruitful. They asked that they might do nothing contrary to the oath of loyalty they had taken to Him, nor in the very least sin against His law of love. They asked that He would keep them in the saving power of His grace, and not allow a single soul to be drawn away to itself and its own merits from that Blood-and-Cross Theology, on which salvation depends. They celebrated the Lord's Supper with hearts at the same time both bowed down and lifted up. Each went home, in great measure lifted up beyond himself, spending this and the following days in great quiet and peace, and learning to love.

A number of children were among those present in the church when the communion was held. One who had been there wrote: "I cannot attribute the great revival among the children to anything else but that wonderful outpouring of the Holy Spirit on the communion assembly. The Spirit breathed in power on old and young. Everywhere they were heard, sometimes at night in the field, beseeching the Saviour to pardon their sins and make them His own. The Spirit of grace had indeed been poured out."

The Brethren frequently went out into the neighborhood to have fellowship with other Christians, and make Christ known to all who would come. When one of them was cast into prison for doing so, it caused great joy that they were found worthy to suffer for His sake.

The Prayer Watch: On August 22nd, it was recorded: "Today, we considered how needful it is that our Church, which is as yet in her infancy and has in Satan such a mighty enemy, should guard herself against one who never slumbers day nor night, and have an unceasing holy watch kept against him. We resolved, therefore, to light a freewill offering of intercession which should burn night and day, leaving the matter for the present to God's working in the hearts of the Brethren. By the 26th the plan had ripened, and twenty-four brethren and twenty-four sisters each engaged to spend an hour, as fixed by lot, in their own rooms, to bring before God all the needs and interests of those around them. The number was soon increased. Since we wished to leave everything in Herrnhut to free grace and have nothing forced, we agreed that when anyone, from poverty of spirit or special business, could not spend the whole hour in prayer, he might instead praise God in spiritual songs, and so bring the sacrifice of praise or of prayer for himself and all saints. These watchers unto prayer met once a week. All news that had been received from far or near concerning the need of persons, congregations, or nations was passed on to them to lead to more hearty and definite prayer and to stir them to praise for answers given.

"In one of the villages we heard of those who wished to come and share in the revival. We instructed these in our discipline with love and humility."

Missions: In the course of the following months some of the Brethren were continually traveling to places near and far, preaching the love of Christ; — their thoughts being continually occupied with the object for which God has so blessed them. The Count kept in contact with all parts of the world, and did not fail to communicate what he heard. At a meeting on the 10th of February 1728 he spoke especially of distant lands — Turkey, Morocco, and Greenland. Of Greenland he said that to all human appearances it looked impossible to gain an entrance; but he believed that the Lord would give our brethren grace and power to visit these countries. It was a day of the Spirit's breathing upon us.

The following four years were times of continual revival. The careful watch kept by the elders and superintendents, and the faithful dealing with individual souls according to personal needs, the jealous maintenance of the spirit of brotherly love, the continual watching unto prayer, the going forth of brethren into other more distant regions with the reports, made the assemblies of the Brethren times of great joy and blessing. This was a time of preparation for the mission work that was to begin.

It came about in this way. In 1731 Count Zinzendorf had gone to Copenhagen to be present at the crowning of the King of Denmark. One of the nobles there had in his service a slave named Anton from the West Indies. From him Zinzendorf heard of the condition of the slaves in the West Indies, specially on St. Thomas, a Danish possession. He also met two Greenland converts of the Danish missionary Egede.

When he returned, the account he gave of meeting these men from unevangelized lands called forth the deepest interest. Two of the Brethren had their hearts touched. In the evening, as the singing bands were passing the home, the Count said to a friend that he believed potential messengers to the West Indies and Greenland would come forth from these brethren, who might offer themselves. When the need became known, two did come forward for Greenland. A visit from Anton, the slave, deepened the impression; and the account of what the slaves suffered, which they also might have to suffer, only made the fire burn more strongly. If it was difficult to approach the plantations to teach the slaves, the volunteers were ready to sell themselves as slaves to reach the poor lost souls.

But it was not until a year later, August 1732, that the two first missionaries left. The instructions with which they were sent out were all comprised in one sentence — to see and be led of the Spirit in all things. They set off on foot, with nothing but a few shillings in their purse, but with strong faith in God and His care. The next year, two left for Greenland. In 1734, eighteen left for Santa Cruz, and in the following year twelve more, to attempt, by establishing settlements and industries, to help the slaves. And though this experiment cost many precious lives and was not a success, the Brethren did not lose courage, but, as the tidings of death came, ever sang the psalm of sowing with tears, and out of the death of the seed, reaped the abundant harvest.

I would like to give at least a short account of the wonderful blessing that marked their work in the West Indies, but space forbids. I must note just one more point in their history. In 1741 an event took place that completed the organization of the church of the Brethren, and set its seal to that which is their chief characteristic — devotion to the Lord Jesus. Leonhard Dober had for some years been the chief elder (the title is really the Eldest) of the Church. He and others felt that his special gifts fitted him more for other work. But as the Brethren in synod looked around, they felt how difficult it would be to find a suitable person to fill his place. At once the thought was suggested to many to ask the Saviour to be the Eldest of His little Church, and in answer to prayer they received the assurance that He would accept the charge. Their one desire was that He would do all that the chief elder had hitherto done and would take them as His special possession, concern Himself about every member individually, and care for all their needs. They promised to love and honor Him, to give Him the confidence of their hearts, to recognize no man as head in the things of the Spirit, and as children to be guided by His mind and will. Of that day on which this decision was made known and accepted at Herrnhut, one wrote: "The 13th of November was the inauguration day of our dear and tenderly beloved Sovereign and Eldest. It was resolved that in honor of our Lord having then condescended to accept this special charge of the Church of His Blood and Cross, there should be a special proclamation of His pardoning grace to all who had wandered away or had fallen. The impression was so intense that at first deep stillness fell upon all, which soon changed into tears of wonder and joy."

It was a new and open profession of the place they had always desired that Christ should have, not only in their theology and their personal life, but especially in their Church. The Church had now become of age.

Not long after this date there came a time of sifting, in which the Brethren appeared to be entering upon a path that might lead to danger. But He to whose guidance the unconditional surrender had been made, did not forsake them, rather He saved them from the threatened evil. The proclamation of Christ as their only Head became the living expression of their hearts' desire that He alone should be all in all.

Let us now turn to the main object for which the story of the Moravian Church has been told. It has been appealed to as an example. It was pointed out to us that in proportion to its membership, the men it supports and sends out, the money it provides, the converts it has gathered, far exceed what any other church has done. In the first twenty years of its existence it actually sent out more missionaries than the whole Protestant Church had done in 200 years. If other churches were to provide men and means in the same proportion, it is believed there would be all that is needed to carry the gospel to every creature.

Let us ask how it happened that this little church, the least of all, had thus outdone all her older and larger sisters? The answer appears to be this: She alone of all the churches has actually sought to carry out the great truth, that *to gather in to Christ the souls He died to save is the one object for which the Church exists.* She alone has sought to teach and train *every one* of her members to count it their first duty to Him who loved them, to give their lives to make Him known to others.

This answer at once leads to the further question: What was it that led and fitted this little church, at a time when she numbered only 300 members, to see and carry out these great truths? It is only as we get some insight into this that we can find out what is needed if other churches are to profit by their example. The closing sentence in Dr. Mott's appeal was: "The practical question is, What has there been in connection with their work already accomplished *which is not reproducible?*" The grace of God that wrought it in them is still exceedingly abundant with faith and love, which are in Christ Jesus.

If we consider Zinzendorf, whom God had so wonderfully prepared to train and guide the young

Church in the path of missions, we see at once what the great moving power was. What marked him above everything was a *tender, childlike, passionate love to our Lord Jesus.* Jesus Christ, the Originator and Inspirer of all mission work, possessed him. The dying love of the Lamb of God had won and filled his heart; the love which had brought Christ to die for sinners had come into his life; he could live for nothing else but to live and, if need be, die for them too. When he took charge of the Moravians, that love, as his teaching and his hymns testify, was the one motive to which he appealed, the one power he trusted, the one object for which he sought to win their lives. The love of Christ did what teaching and argument and discipline, however necessary and fruitful, never could have done. It melted all into one body; it made all willing to be corrected and instructed; it made all long to put away everything that was sin; it inspired all with the desire to testify of Jesus; it made many ready to sacrifice all in making that love known to others, and so making the heart of Jesus glad.

If the dying love of Christ were to take the place in our churches and their teaching, in our own hearts and fellowship with each other, which it had in theirs, which it has in God's heart and in Christ's redemption, would it not work a mighty change in our mission work?

Along with this love to Christ, or rather, as the fruit of it, there was in Zinzendorf an intense sense of *the need and the value of fellowship.* He believed that love, to be enjoyed and to grow strong, and to attain its object, needs expression and communication. He believed that the love of Christ in us needs fellowship with each other for its maintenance in ourselves, as well as for the securing of God's great purpose in it — the comforting and strengthening of our brethren. So he was prepared to take up the strangers God brought to him, and give himself wholly to them. His reward was great. He was able to give himself to them, and *to find himself multiplied in each one.* What he said later, "I know of no true Christianity without fellowship," was the principle that begat that intense unity which gave the strength of the leader and the whole body to each of its members.

In our modern religion there is a reticence in speaking of our personal relationship to Jesus which often causes great loss. We forget that the majority of men are guided more by emotions than by intellect: *the heart is the great power* by which they are meant to be influenced and moulded. We might well take a lesson here from Zinzendorf.

A minister with his congregation, a teacher with his class, a leader in a prayer-meeting or a youth group, often works hard to influence by instruction and encouragement, while he forgets that hearts crave love, and that nothing can so help to build up the young or weak Christian life as the warm fellowship of love in Christ. There are thousands of Christians, wishing to serve their Lord, but not knowing how, who are just longing to find gatherings where they can be helped to meet under a sense of the presence of our Lord Jesus and His love — where they can be helped to confess that love, and then to yield themselves to it in the faith that it will constrain and enable them *to do anything their Lord needs them to do.*

At the Conference it was well said by one speaker: "*The importance of leadership* must be emphasized. Let us put to work that talent which sets another to work. The leader must use definiteness and persistence. The leader must uplift ideals. To be the leader is the responsibility of the pastor. Come to us with the deepest spiritual note you can sound, and we will follow you."

And by another: "We shall need devoted pastors to lead in the execution of this work. The pastors are still the leaders. If they only will, they may be the leaders in this holy war for righteousness in all the earth."

And by still another: "Men become interested not so much in abstract ideas as in individuals who represent their ideas. Victories are won because men follow some leader whom they have learned to love."

Zinzendorf was indeed a mighty leader, in whose footsteps we still may follow. Every pastor may learn from him the great secret, that the more intensely the fire of God's love burns in the heart, the more surely will it burn into those around us. It is the high privilege of every leader to know that God can give him such power over others, that their love to him can open their hearts for receiving more of the life and love and power of God than they could have had without him. God's way is to dispense His blessings through individual men.

As each leader in his circle realizes his privilege of being filled with the missionary fire, the love and devotion of Christ Jesus, and then living up to it, missionary work at home will enter a new era. Life and love, passing from the living, loving Christ, through a living, loving disciple, will communicate life and love to those who otherwise are cold and helpless.

What of the followers God had provided for the leader? What especially qualified them to take the lead among the churches of the Reformation?

Let their history give the answer. There was first of all that detachment from the world and its hopes, that power of endurance, that simple trust in God, which affliction and persecution are meant to work. These men were literally strangers and pilgrims on earth. They were familiar with the thought and spirit of sacrifice. They had learned to endure hardship, and to look up to God in every trouble.

It is this spirit which is still needed in the Church. A disregard of what the world considers necessary or desirable; a self-denial that counts all but loss for the sake of knowing Christ and making Him known; a trust in God that looks not only to His aid in special emergency, but for His guidance at every step and His power in every work; these were certainly the elements that went far to form Zinzendorf's "Warrior Band," and that still make good soldiers of Christ.

The discipline which they had inherited from their ancestors, and to which they were led to yield themselves so completely at Herrnhut was rooted in the view that, to the Christian, faith is the all-important thing. Everything is secondary to the one great consideration — to know and do the will of God, to walk in the footsteps of Jesus

Christ. For the sake of this they were ready to submit to the care and correction of all those appointed to watch over them. Believing literally in the command, "Exhort one another daily," they were willing to be reproved or warned as often as there was sin, either of omission or commission. When they were sent out, they were ready to help, to depend upon, and to yield to each other. Their fellowship made them strong: the highest in rule begged his brethren to tell what they might see wrong in him and he was willing to confess the slightest shortcoming. The spirit of subjection to one another, of which Scripture speaks so often, brought its rich blessing in sanctifying and strengthening the whole life.

To introduce the same discipline in our day may appear impossible. But the same spirit of watchful care of, and loving subjection to, one another is still within the reach of any circle that will seek for it, and will still be a wonderful preparation for effective work in God's kingdom.

But there was still something more than this which gave their fellowship its wonderful power. It was the intensity of their united and personal devotion to Jesus Christ, as the Lamb of God, who had purchased them with His blood. All their correction of each other, and their willing confession and giving up of sin, came from this faith in the living Christ, through whom they found "within their hearts the peace of God and deliverance from the power of sin." This faith led them to accept and jealously keep their place as poor sinners, saved by His grace, every day. This faith — cultivated and strengthened every day by fellowship in word and song and prayer — became the food of their life. This faith filled them with such joy that their hearts rejoiced, in the midst of the greatest difficulties, in the triumphant assurance that their Jesus, the Lamb who had died for them, and was now loving and saving and keeping them hour by hour, could conquer the hardest heart, and was willing to bless the vilest sinner. In this spirit they met together for nearly five years, from the time of the first outpouring of the Spirit to the time the first missionaries went out. They continued worshipping the Son of God, offering themselves to Him, and waiting for Him to make known what He would have of His Church, each one holding himself in readiness to go or do what his Lord should show.

Let a congregation, a prayer meeting, or a Christian circle seek to have this kind of spirit uniting the members, while all continue in prayer that the Lord would show each one His blessed will for them, and you have the beginning of a spirit that will spread. And as different congregations combine in making the worship and faith of the Lord Jesus and devotion to Him the center of their missionary interest, the number of those who are ready to go forth will speedily increase.

There is one thing more we must notice — the mighty moving of the Holy Spirit in answer to prayer. We have had the Count's testimony of how confident he was that the birth of the new Church, on the 12th of May 1727, was the work of the Spirit. We have read of the overwhelming sense of the Holy Spirit presence in which she received her baptism from on high. Many a time after this during the following four years the records testify of special experiences of the deep movings of the Holy Spirit. This was mostly when they were gathered in prayer before their Lord, the slain Lamb. The prayer watch they appointed, so as to keep up day and night a continual sacrifice of supplication, proves what they understood Heaven's first law to be — that the measure of blessing and power will depend upon the measure of prayer. They saw and rejoiced exceedingly in the Lamb upon the Throne — of course they could trust Him to fill their mouths and hearts so widely opened to Him.

As at Pentecost, so at Herrnhut, united prayer, rewarded with the gift of the Spirit, was the entrance into the life of witness and victory. *It is the law of all mission work.* If the example of the Moravian Brethren is to stir us to jealousy, we must learn, from them, what it is to believe that we only exist to win the souls for Jesus He died to save. Then we must train our members to the thought that *everyone* must be ready for His service. We must learn the lesson of much prayer and of a definite surrender to have our whole lives under the leading of the Holy Spirit.

When we point to the example of the Brethren, the question is sometimes asked whether they have retained their first fire, whether their missionaries and members are still living on a higher spiritual level than the churches around them. The answer is very simple. Like every other church, the Brethren have had their times of decline and revival. They were too closely one with the church around them not to suffer with it when the cold of winter came. The force of our appeal is not weakened however, but strengthened by this fact. Its point is this: The three great principles taught by the Holy Spirit in any time of His mighty working are these: (1) that the Church exists only for extending the kingdom, (2) that every member must be trained to take part in it, and (3) that the personal experience of the love of Christ is the power that fits for this. To these principles the Brethren have remained true, and it is in this respect that their example speaks to us with such power.

The Church of Christ owes more to the Moravians than is generally known. From her John Wesley received that joyful assurance of acceptance which gave his preaching such power, and fitted him as God's instrument, not only to found the Wesleyan Church, but to take such an important part in the revival of evangelical faith in England. William Carey owed part of his inspiration for the missionary cause to them. When pleading with his brethren, he backed his proposals by the experience of the Moravians, and laid upon the table early numbers of their *Periodical Accounts.* His companion, William Ward, recorded the profound impression produced on his mind by these *Accounts,* and exclaimed, "Thank you, Moravians! You have done me good. If I am ever a missionary worth a straw, I shall, under our Saviour, owe it to you." The story of the wondrous grace of God in the Moravians may still show us the path, and inspire the courage, to seek and find new blessing for the world.

4

The Deepening of Spiritual Life

Closely connected to missionary motivation is the deepening of spiritual life. The Conference frequently referred to the Church Missionary Society in England as a worthy example. During a short period of twelve years, its income was raised from two hundred thousand to three hundred thousand pounds and the number of workers more than tripled.

Eugene Stock gave the background:

In 1887 the Church Missionary Society, under special circumstances, passed the resolution not to refuse on financial grounds any candidate for a foreign field who appeared to be God-called. This was not on the basis of excitement or gush, but on the plain, simple, business principle that if God calls a person, He will provide for him. I truly believe that the Lord will find the money. If, as far as man can judge, a certain man or woman is called of God to go, we have a right then to pray, 'O Lord, we look to Thee to enable us to send this person.'

If anyone had said to us on that memorable day, when we were all on our knees in prayer on this subject, 'You will triple your force in thirteen years,' our response would have been, 'There will be no money to send them. It is impossible!' *But the impossible thing has been done,* the staff has tripled, and the money has been found. God sent it.

Let me remind you of this: I do not care what Christian enterprise it is, even simply saying a word in season to your brother, in your bank, in your office, in your store — it is not an easy thing to do, is it? If it is only to say a kind word for Jesus to some young girl whom you know is going in the wrong direction and you want to rescue her from danger — is it an easy thing? Some would say, 'I cannot.' Whether it is a little thing like that, or whether it is the great work of all the mission boards and societies in America going in for a policy of faith in the Lord, I want you to write over any of these enterprises three mottoes: First — imagine it written in letters of fire across this hall, 'With men it is impossible.' Second, 'With God all things are possible.' And third, 'All things are possible to him that believeth.'

Perhaps you will hardly believe it when I tell you what the constituency of the Church Missionary Society is. You may think it is very large. No, it does not comprise one-fourth of the Church of England and not more than one-fourth of our congregations give any support to our Society. We are the largest society even though we represent but a small section of the Church. Why is that? It is because of the enthusiasm of praying people. It is because of the enthusiasm of those who believe that, outside of all organizations, the gospel of Christ is the power of God and of salvation. We hold to the rightful independence of any Christians to band themselves together to teach the gospel as the Lord shall teach them.

When we consider what has been done by the Moravian Church or the Church of Pentecost, the thought may be that these belong to the past. The C.M.S. gives its witness as to what God is doing under our very eyes in awakening His people to do what otherwise appeared impossible, by enabling them to give men and money to an extent unknown before. If we are really to profit by this lesson, and to labor that the whole Church will give to God what He asks for in the extension of His kingdom, let us inquire in what way the C.M.S. was led to the great increase of blessing and of labor.

The centenary history of the Society tells the story. It proves that, as much as we need to pray for the power of the Holy Spirit upon missionaries and their work, we need to pray for the *leaders* of mission work, and for the *churches* which support them, that all devising of means and methods, that all appeals for men and money, that all meetings for awakening interest or uniting prayer, may be in true dependence on the power of the Holy Spirit. In the long run the spiritual tone of the missionaries and the mission congregation abroad cannot be higher than that of the home church out of which it was born. Certainly it is of great importance that the efforts of Mission Societies or Boards on behalf of the unevangelized, and the messengers sent out to them, be in divine power. No less important is the work of quickening and raising the spiritual standard of the church at home with its members and ministers so that their interest and aid in the work may equally be in the power of the Spirit.

The principal lesson the C.M.S. history teaches is that its great forward movement was *intimately connected with a deep revival of spiritual life, and the teaching of a higher standard of devotion to the Lord Jesus.* The only way to waken true, deep, spiritual, permanent missionary interest, is not to aim at this itself, so much as to lead believers to a more complete separation from the world, and to an entire consecration of themselves, with all they have, to their Lord and His service.

The movement is traced back to 1882, when D. L. Moody's visit to Cambridge resulted in the powerful conversion of a number of students.

There are devoted clergymen and laymen, both at home and abroad, who owe 'their own selves' to that visit of Mr. Moody. The C.M.S. owes a whole succession of missionaries to the influences of that period ... One of the most important results of Moody's work, was the going forth of the famous 'Cambridge Seven.' The influence of such a band of men going to China as missionaries was irresistible. No such event had occurred before, and no event of the century has done so much to arouse the minds of Christians to the claims and the nobility of the missionary vocation. The gift of such a band — for truly it was a gift from God — was a just reward to Mr. Hudson Taylor and his colleagues for their genuine unselfishness. They had always pleaded the cause of China and the world, and not of their own particular organization.

Consequently a deep spirituality had always marked their meetings. And that same spirituality marked most emphatically the densely crowded meetings in different places at which these seven men said farewell. They told, modestly and yet fearlessly, of the Lord's goodness to them, and of their joy in serving Him. They appealed to young men, *not for their own Mission, but for their Divine Master.* No such missionary meetings had ever been known as the farewell gathering at Exeter Hall on February 4th, 1885. We have become familiar since then with meetings more or less of the same type, but it was a new thing then. In many ways the C.M.S. owes a deep debt of gratitude to the China Inland Mission and the Cambridge Seven. The Lord Himself spoke through them, and it was by His grace that the Society had ears to hear.

The next influence related to the C.M.S. was that of the Keswick deeper life Conventions in England. God was preparing the way for the accomplishment of His plans. For the first few years of its existence, the Keswick Conventions had no direct connection with missions. When Reginald Radcliffe pleaded for their admission to the program, all he could obtain was the loan of the tent on a Saturday. At the next year's meeting an appeal by a C.M.S. missionary, asking for Christian ladies with their own support to come as missionaries to the Holy Land, touched many hearts. By another year the Chairman of the Convention had grasped and enunciated the great principle *that personal consecration and the evangelization of the world ought to go together,* and missionary meetings were included in the official program. At the Saturday meeting of that year a £10 note given by a young man "to help to send out a Keswick missionary" helped to lay the foundation of the fund from which Keswick missionaries have been sent forth, and missionaries in connection with different societies supported.

To go on with the history of the Society, the year 1885 was a memorable one. In January 1885 the usual Annual Conference of the Association Secretaries was held at the Church Missionary Home.

At that Conference the spiritual character of the meetings held by Mr. Hudson Taylor and his Cambridge recruits was referred to, and the idea of arranging special gatherings simultaneously in different centers to present the claims, not of the Society, but of the devotion of His servants, was not warmly welcomed at first. There was somewhat of a feeling that it was rather beneath the dignity of the 'grand old Society' to copy the China Inland Mission! But this suggestion later bore fruit in the February Simultaneous Meetings in 1886 and 1887.

A weekly prayer meeting was begun in the Church Missionary Home. Some doubted whether it would be possible to keep it up regularly, but a historian has written: "After fourteen years' experience, who would stop it now? What should we do without it? Only in eternity shall we know what the Society owes to the Thursday prayer meetings."

In the same month, in Exeter Hall, a few weeks after the great farewell meeting for the Cambridge band, another meeting for men was held, sponsored by the Y.M.C.A. to give the C.M.S. the opportunity for presenting the cause of missions. The historian writes:

In one respect the meeting marked the beginning of a new aim in missionary meetings. For the first time the Society's name did not head the promotion. The heading was centered upon the needs of the unevangelized world. A small thing in itself, but it was the token of a revolution. From that time the C.M.S. has tried to raise its meetings above the level of collecting money for a Society; indeed the whole missionary cause in the world has been lifted by that simple change to a higher platform. But let it not be forgotten that the example had already been set by Hudson Taylor and the China Inland Mission. Dr. Handley Moule's words were memorable: 'There never should be a missionary meeting that is not full of the presence of the Lord. Do we not all feel it here tonight? What has gathered us together here? Not the annual invitation, *but the movement of the Spirit of God visibly in the world and in the Church.* We are indeed at a time when God is making Himself felt in the spirit, in the life, in the faith, and in the work of men, not with new energy, for it is always the same, but in ways in which we can trace His blessed hand with special clearness.

'We are not here tonight to praise the Church of England, nor the C.M.S. We are in the presence of our Divine King; let us concentrate our thoughts upon Him and upon His will. God's demand upon every one of His servants is surrender with no conditions, no terms; nothing but the yielding of our will and of our life to Him to do His will in the strength of His might. In the old feudal days, when the vassal did his homage to his lord, he did this: he put his hands together, and put them within the hands of his lord, in token of absolute submission to his will and readiness for activity in his work. *That is the only true position for a Christian's hands,* the hands and heart and will, the spirit and life. Not one hand but both, completely within the hands of the Sovereign, the infinitely more than feudal Lord, the Despot, the glorious, absolute, unconstitutional Despot of His servants, the infinitely trustworthy, infinitely sovereign Lord Jesus Christ.'

Then Dr. Moule went on to specifically challenge the students at the meeting: 'For you young men who are here in such multitudes, this is not merely a great and interesting occasion; you are here before the unseen, the real, the personal Lord Jesus Christ. He is here! He is now speaking to you through this meeting as His voice; and you must say something to Him, whatever it is, in reply. Are you prepared to live for His service, whether at home or abroad, whether in the commonest round of the most ordinary life till you die, or in the high places of the field? Are you prepared to live as those who have put their hands into His, and have recognized distinctly that the center of your life is shifted from self to Jesus Christ; that you have distinctly laid down at His feet all those desires which attract notice for self's sake, to get praise, even the least item, that is generated by self? You belong to Him if you are His; you are to live as those that belong to Him. All your gains are to go into your master's purse, and He is to decide where, and how, and how long you are to serve.

Dr. Moule's message was reinforced by the exquisite hymn he wrote at that very time—

> *My glorious Victory, prince Divine,*
> *Clasp these surrendered hands in Thine.*
> *At length my will is all Thine own,*
> *Glad vassal of a Saviour's throne!*

The movement for the deepening of spiritual life at Keswick was indeed very closely allied to the quickening of the missionary spirit in the Society. It proclaims as with trumpet voice the great truth, that, if the Church is to be aroused to do her duty towards the evangelization of the world, *there must not only be the missionary appeal, but a living experience of the Spirit's power.* If these two are solidly linked, it will equip the speakers for appealing to the right motive, and the Christian Church for yielding to it personal and wholehearted devotion to Jesus Christ and His service.

From the history of the C.M.S. we have this stirring summary: "We have learned in our long survey that *missionary advance depends upon spiritual life.* Evangelical Orthodoxy is powerless in itself to spread the gospel. Unimpeachable Protestant teaching in the pulpit, and the plainest of gospel declaration in the church services, may be seen in combination with entire neglect of the Lord's great commission. But if the Holy Ghost Himself stirs the hearts and enlightens the eyes, then the conversion of the unconverted becomes a matter of anxious concern. We have seen how much the modern development of missions owes to the Spirit's movements of the day. Consecration and the evangelization of the world go together. The latter depends upon the former. The missionary impulse of a hundred years ago sprang from the Methodist Revival; the early German missionaries were the fruit of the Pietist movement on the Continent; the recent growth of missionary zeal in the Church of England is due in no small degree to the influence of an American evangelist, and a free-lance China missionary, neither of them a member of the Church of England. God has shown us that He is sovereign, and that He works according to His will, sometimes by means of the most unlikely instruments — *because it has pleased Him to fill those instruments with His Spirit!"*

God does not stereotype movements and methods through which He sends blessing. But He wants His children in each case to learn what the secret source of the blessing was. What was the power in the case of the Keswick Convention, and the blessing it brought? The answer may be found in the expression — the deepening of the spiritual life.

No one can understand the value of Keswick who does not give full weight to the deep sense in many believers of a lack in the spiritual life, and the faith that a definite deepening and strengthening of it is possible. The consciousness of that lack was generally felt in connection with the painful experience of the power of sin in daily life. The memoirs of the originator of the convention, Canon T.D. Harford - Battersby, and of one of its latest and youngest leaders, Rev. G. H. C. McGregor, both prove this. They were men of marked godliness in life and devotion to their Master's work. But there was always a secret dissatisfaction and self-condemnation. How was it, they asked, that temper, selfishness and worldliness so often gain the upper hand and robbed the soul of its peace? All their struggles and prayers appeared vain; deliverance seemed impossible.

They heard men testify of having once been in the same state; then having found that it was because of their not knowing Christ's full power to save. They were told that there was a deliverance from the power of sin which Christ can give, not by the removal of the sinful taint from one's nature, but by His own presence and keeping power. As they listened they saw how little they had believed in that *power of Christ as a real continual experience.* They saw in God's Word that it was what Christ could do and would do, and that nothing was needed on their part but a new — and now, in the assurance that He would equip them, a full — surrender to His keeping and service. They yielded, they believed, they entrusted themselves to Him in a way they had never done before, and they testified that Christ was faithful and brought them into a life of communion, of peace and strength in His own keeping that they had never known previously. It was the living testimony of these and many others that gave the Keswick platform its wonderful attractiveness and power. Men stood there as living witnesses to the power of Christ to save from the power of sin in daily life.

Around the three words, *Sin, Faith, Consecration* the whole Keswick teaching continually circles. Deep conviction of sin was often the first sign that the teaching was laying hold. George McGregor wrote from Keswick, "I have learned innumerable lessons, principally these: My own sinfulness and shortcoming — I have been searched through and through, and bared and exposed by God's light. Then I have learned the unsearchableness of Christ — how Christ is magnified here, you can have scarcely any idea. And I have learned the absolute necessity of obedience — given obedience and faith, nothing is impossible."

Speaking of McGregor's nervous temperament, mainfesting itself in quick temper, and his thought that it was a cross to be borne, his biographer wrote: "At Keswick he learned to think differently about this. There he learned, as never before, to understand that yielding to any evil tendency, however deeply rooted in one's nature, were it hereditary twenty times over, is SIN. And God does not mean His children to live in any kind of sin, or to yield to sin. He calls men to holiness, and when He so calls He does not mock them by impossiblities. In his time of self-abasement at Keswick, McGregor had a special sense of evil and made a special confession to God of his besetting sin of temper. When after these days of consecration he left Keswick, to a large extent the evil temper was left behind. From that time he was really, in this respect, a different man."

Paul wrote of the Corinthians that, because there was among them strife and division, they were still carnal and not spiritual. One chief mark of the desire to be truly spiritual is the desire not to sin, to be delivered from the common sins of which the average Christian is so tolerant. When this desire ripens into faith the person is brought into an altogether fresh and much clearer consciousness of Christ's power to save, and learns how broad and deep is the meaning of faith. He then lives by the faith of Him who loved and gave Himself, and now lives in us, and is Himself our keeper. What has this to do with missions? The new experience of what Christ has done for *oneself* leads to a larger trust in what He can do *for others*. This gives a point and a courage in testifying of Him, which brings a new tone into a person's preaching or speaking. Christ becomes more distinctly the center of all thought and all work; at the same time the source, the subject, the strength of all our witness. With this, the claim of Christ and His service upon our devotion and loyalty and entire surrender becomes clearer. It is seen that entire consecration, which at conversion was hardly understood, is both our simple duty and our highest privilege. And work for Christ, or rather a life wholly given up to live for Him and for the souls He loves, becomes the unceasing aim of the liberated soul.

In its teaching of these truths Keswick is naturally led to lay emphasis on the mighty saving power of Christ, on the sin of limiting Him, on the call to honor Him by an unbounded trust, and on His claims to a life wholly devoted to His will and service. The transition from the thought of faith and consecration as related to personal blessing, to their application in a life given up to winning souls to the Saviour, is simple and sure. Many have found that what at first was sought for the sake of *personal blessing,* becomes the power for living *to be a blessing to others.* So the deepening of the Christian life becomes the power of a new devotion to missions and the Kingdom of our Lord.

That is what the story of the C.M.S. teaches. This is the lesson the whole Church of Christ may learn from it in her search for the key to the missionary problem. Many can never attend a Convention. It may appear difficult or impossible to move our large churches or societies simultaneously, so as to get the life really deepened and fitted for the tremendous work that has been undertaken in this generation. Let the beginning be made with single congregations. Let the pastor learn and teach that all failure in caring, giving, praying and living for missions, is owing to *a weak, superficial spiritual life.* Let him call upon his people to follow him as he seeks to lead them to a deeper spiritual life. Let him speak of sin, and Christ as a Saviour from it; of faith in Christ as able to do more than we have experienced or expected; of entire consecration, the giving up of our will and all we have, to be wholly under the control of our Lord, as the only door to abiding happiness and true service.

Let the pastor plead with his people, by the love and honor of Christ, by the need of the unevangelized, by the inconceivable privilege of being made the channel of the divine life to the souls of men, to come and be whole-hearted for Christ. Let him speak of work for Christ among those near or far as the one thing by which we can prove our faith and love. Let him gather the people to pray for the Holy Spirit's working in themselves to equip them for mission work. Let him encourage the faith that, if hearts give themselves in simplicity to their Lord, expecting His guidance, He will show what He would have them do. As both the deepening of the spirit life and devotion to mission work are sought after, the one will react on the other, because both have their root in Jesus

Christ Himself, revealed afresh as Saviour and Lord.

When such a new revelation of Christ takes place, a new relationship is established. Prayer becomes the spontaneous turning of the believer, or of a company of believers, to Him who has proved His power to them. They know that the power will come from Him for all they have to do, and on all the work that is done. For the sad complaint of lack of time or heart for much prayer, for the vain call to more prayer, *there is but one cure — the deepening of the spiritual life.* The missionary problem is a personal one. Lead men to the deliverance there is in Christ. Lead them from the half-hearted, worldly life in which they have lived, back to the "first love" of a personal attachment and devotion to the living, loving Christ. Then they will see that there is no life worth living but that of devotion to His kingdom. Prayer, private and public, will flow, and the blessing it draws down from heaven will prepare the Church to labor as it has never yet done, and to see blessing above all we can ask or think.

Yes, the missionary problem is a personal one. *Seek the deepening of the spiritual life, and missionary consecration will follow.*

5

The Power of
Believing Prayer

In the New York Conference, the China Inland Mission* was frequently mentioned. Under the leadership of one man of faith, God had, in the course of thirty years, led out 600 missionaries into the field, without any guarantee of funds for their support beyond what God might give in answer to believing prayer. We have already seen how strongly the historian of the C.M.S. speaks of the blessing that that society owes to the China Inland Mission in stirring it to give the policy of faith a large place in its work. If the Church at large is to profit by the example, it is well that all Christians who take part in the support of missions should know what was the secret of its power. It is not necessary to copy its methods and organization. But there is urgent need

*The present *Overseas Missionary Fellowship*

everywhere throughout the Church of learning how the power of God can be brought into our mission work.

At the New York Conference Hudson Taylor spoke of the source of power for Christian missions, and gave an example of what the power of believing prayer is. I quote at some length from his speech:

God Himself is the great source of power. Furthermore, God's power is available power. We are a supernatural people, born again by a supernatural birth, kept by a supernatural power, sustained on supernatural food, taught by a supernatural Teacher from a supernatural Book. We are led by a supernatural Captain in right paths to assured victories. The risen Saviour, before He ascended on high, said to His disciples, 'Ye shall receive power when the Holy Ghost is come upon you.' Not many days after this, in answer to united and continued prayer, the Holy Ghost did come upon them, and they were all filled. Praise God, He remains with us still. The power given is *not a gift* from the Holy Ghost. *He, Himself, is the power.* Today, He is as truly available and as mighty in power as He was on the day of Pentecost. But has the whole Church ever, since the days before Pentecost, put aside every other work and waited for Him for ten days, so that power might be manifested? Has there not been a source of failure here?

We have given too much attention to methods and to machinery and to resources, and too little to the source of power — the filling with the Holy Ghost. This, I think you will agree with me, is the great weakness today, and has been the great weakness of our service in the past. Unless remedied, it will be the great weakness in the future. We are commanded to be filled with the Spirit. If we are not filled, we are living in disobedience and sin, and the cause of our sin is the cause of Israel's sin of old — the sin of unbelief.

It is not lost time to wait upon God. May I refer to a small gathering of about a dozen men in which I was permitted to take part, in November 1886. We, in the China Inland Mission, were feeling greatly the need of Divine guidance in the matters of organization and reinforcement in the field. We came together before our conference to spend eight days in united waiting upon God, four alternate days being days of fasting as well as prayer. We were led to pray for a hundred missionaries to be sent out by our English Board during 1887. In connection with our Forward Movement, we needed to ask God for $50,000, in addition to the income of the previous year. We were guided to pray that this might be given in large sums, so that our staff might not be unduly occupied in the acknowledgement of contributions.

What was the result? God sent us offers of service from over six hundred men and women during the following year, and those considered ready and suitable were accepted and sent out to China. At the end of the year exactly one hundred had gone! Further, God did not give us exactly the $50,000 we asked for, but He gave us $55,000 which came in eleven contributions: the smallest was $2500, the largest was $12,500. We had a thanksgiving for the men and the money.

The power of the living God is available power. We may call upon Him in the name of Christ, with the assurance that if we are taught by the Spirit in our prayers, those prayers will be answered.

Where and how had the secret of such believing prayer been learned? Was it a gift bestowed by divine favor on a chosen one, which others cannot expect to receive? Or was it the result of training and practicing, the reward of faithfulness in little things, to teach us that we, too, can walk in the same path? It was indeed a gift, as every grace is a gift of God bestowed in different measure as He pleases. But it was at the same time the outcome of a life of trial and obedience, by which the gift that had been only a little, hidden, unconscious seed had been developed. It had grown strong so that all God's children might be encouraged to walk in his footsteps, with the assurance that to each one, in his measure, the path of prevailing prayer stands open. Listen to the story of how Hudson Taylor learned it:

Not many months after my conversion, having a leisure afternoon, I retired to my room to spend it largely in communion with God. Well do I remember that occasion. In the gladness of my heart, I poured out my soul before God. Again and again, I confessed my grateful love to Him who had done everything for me. God had saved me when I had given up all hope and even wish for salvation. I asked Him to give me some work to do for Him as an outlet for my love and gratitude: some self-denying service, no matter what it might be, however trying or however trivial. I asked for something with which He would be pleased and that I might do directly for Him who had done so much for me.

Well do I remember, as in unreserved consecration I put myself, my life, my friends, my all upon the altar, the deep solemnity that came over my soul with the assurance that my offering was accepted. The presence of God became unutterably real and blessed. Though I was only a boy of fifteen, I remember stretching myself on the ground, and lying there silent before Him with unspeakable awe and unspeakable joy. For what service I was accepted I did not know; but a deep consciousness that I was no longer my own took possession of me, which has never since left me. Within a few months of this time of consecration the impression came into my soul that the Lord wanted me in China.

Consecration is always the outcome of a powerful conversion, and the secret of a life in which power in prayer and faith are to be acquired. Some are inclined to look upon it as an attainment and an end: *Its true value consists in its being a beginning,* a putting oneself into God's hands to prepare for His service. It is only the entrance into the higher class of the school where God Himself teaches how He desires us to serve.

Hudson Taylor still had much to learn before he could become the man of faith who could be a witness to what God can do. In thinking of going to China he felt that he wanted to do so in faith, trusting God for the supply of his needs. If he was to trust Him in China, why not learn to trust Him in England? Failure in China might be fatal: he would ask God to teach him at home how to walk in faith. He understood the command, "owe no man anything," to be meant literally: however great his need might be, he would speak to none but God about it. Two stories out of his experience at this time show the schooling through which his faith was trained.

My kind employer, busily occupied, wished me to remind him when my salary became due. I determined to ask God to remind him of it, and so encourage me by answering prayer. At the end of a certain quarter, when my salary was due, one Saturday night I found that I had only a single coin, one half-crown piece. Still I had hitherto had no lack, and I continued in prayer.

That Sunday was a very happy one. After Divine service in the morning, the rest of the day was filled with gospel work as usual in lodging-houses in the lowest part of the town. It seemed as though heaven had begun below. After my last service at ten o'clock that night, a poor man asked me to go and pray with his wife, as she was dying, and the priest had refused to come without a payment of one shilling and sixpence. The man could not produce this because the family was starving. It flashed into my mind at once that all the money I possessed was the solitary half-crown, and that it was in one coin. Moreover, though I had porridge sufficient for supper and for breakfast, I had nothing for dinner the next day.

At once there was a stoppage of the flow of joy in my heart. Instead of reproving myself, I began to reprove the poor man. I found he had applied to the relief officer, and had been told to come at eleven the next morning; but he feared his wife might not live through the night. 'Ah,' thought I, 'if only I had two shillings and a sixpence instead of this half-crown, how gladly would I give these poor people one shilling!' The truth of the matter was that I could trust God plus one shilling and six-pence, but could not trust Him only, without any money.

The poor man led me into a court where, on my last visit, I had been roughly handled. I followed up a miserable flight of stairs, and into a wretched room, and oh! what a sight presented itself to us! Four or five starved-looking children stood about, and on a wretched pallet lay the poor mother, with a tiny babe, thirty-six hours old, moaning at her side. 'Ah,' thought I, 'if I had two shillings and a sixpence instead of half a crown, how gladly would I give one shilling and sixpence of it.' Still unbelief prevented me from relieving their distress at the cost of all I possessed.

Strange to say, I could not comfort these poor people. I told them not to be cast down, for they had a kind, loving Father in heaven; but something said to me, 'You hypocrite, speaking about a kind, loving Father when you are not prepared to trust Him without half a crown!' I nearly choked. If I had only had a florin and a sixpence! — but I was not yet ready to trust God without the sixpence.

In those days prayer was usually a delight to me; so I tried to pray, but when I opened my lips with 'Our Father which art in heaven,' prayer seemed a mockery, and I passed through such a time of conflict as I have never experienced before or since. I arose from my knees in great distress.

The poor father turned to me and said, 'Sir, if you can help us, for God's sake, do!' and the word flashed into my mind, 'Give to him that asketh of thee' and 'in the word of a king there is power'. Slowly taking the halfcrown from my pocket, I gave it to the man, saying that I was giving him my all, but that God was really a Father and might be trusted. All the joy came back to my heart, and the hindrance to blessing was gone — gone, I trust, for ever.

Not only was the woman's life saved, but I was saved too. My Christian life might have been a wreck had the striving of God's Spirit not been obeyed. As I went home, my heart as light as my pocket, the lonely streets resounded with a hymn of praise. As I knelt at my bedside, I reminded the Lord that 'he who giveth to the poor lendeth to the Lord'; and with peace within and peace without, I spent a restful night.

Next morning, at breakfast, I was surprised to see my landlady come in with a letter in her hand. I could not recognize the handwriting or the postmark, and where it came from I could not tell. On opening the envelope I found, inside a sheet of blank paper, a pair of kid gloves, and as I opened them, half a sovereign fell to the ground. 'Praise the Lord!' I exclaimed; 'four hundred percent for twelve hours' investment! How glad the merchants would be to lend their money at such a rate!' Then and there I determined that a bank which could not break should have my savings — a determination I have not yet learned to regret.

A second trial of faith occurred some days later.

This remarkable deliverance was a great joy to me, but still ten shillings will not go very far, and the larger sum still remained due to me. I continued pleading with God that He would graciously remind my employer that my salary was overdue. It was not the want of money that troubled me, but the thought in my mind was this: 'Can I go to China or will my lack of faith prove an obstacle to this much-prized service?'

When Saturday evening came, a payment was due to my landlady. Ought I not, for her sake, to speak about the salary? I gave much time on Thursday and Friday to earnest wrestling in prayer with God, and by Saturday morning I received an assurance that to wait God's time was best. So I waited, my heart at rest and the burden gone.

That afternoon, as I was watching a pan in which a decoction was boiling, the doctor came in from his rounds, and, as was his custom, began to speak of the things of God. Suddenly, without any introduction, he said, 'By the bye, Taylor, is not your salary due again?' My emotion may be imagined! I told him, as quietly as I could, that it was overdue for some little time. How thankful I felt! God had surely heard my prayer. Presently he continued, 'I am so sorry you did not remind me, for I sent all the money I had to the bank this afternoon; otherwise I would pay you at once.' It is impossible to describe my feeling of revulsion, and I was glad to get away without the doctor perceiving my emotion.

I then sought my little sanctum, and poured out my heart before the Lord, until calmness and joy were restored to me. I felt that God was going to work in His own way.

That evening was spent in preparing for my work for the next day, and it was about ten o'clock before I got ready to go home. There seemed no help for that night; perhaps on Monday God would interpose for me. Just as I was leaving, I heard the doctor come in, laughing heartily to himself. Entering the surgery, he asked for his ledger, telling me that one of his richest patients had just been to pay his bill — was it not an odd thing to do? I, too, was highly amused that a man rolling in wealth should come so late to pay a bill which might any time have been paid by a check. The account was duly receipted in the ledger, and the doctor about to leave, when he suddenly handed me some of the bank-notes, saying, 'By the way, Taylor, you might as well take these notes, and I can give you the balance next week.' Again I was left to go back to my own little closet to praise the Lord with a joyful heart that, after all, I might go to China.

These two incidents prove what training is needed in private before men are allowed in public to become witnesses to the power of faith in God and the prevailing prayer which brings it about. They teach us that, if our public united mission work is really to be a work in which the power of believing prayer is to be displayed, the faith of individual believers must have its roots deeply fixed in true consecration to God, and in entire dependence upon His mighty power working through us.

In 1854 Taylor left England for China. After laboring for five years he was compelled to return home because of ailing health. During his stay at home he prayed much for five laborers to go to Ningpo where he had been stationed. Part of the time was spent in bringing out a revised New Testament with references, in the dialect of the people among whom he had lived. He tells how, in doing this work, he only thought of the use it would be to the Chinese Christians. He discovered later on, that, had it not been for that time of close encounter with God's Word, he would have been quite unprepared to form a mission like the C.I.M.

"In the study of that divine Word I learned that to obtain successful workers, what was needed was not elaborate appeals for help, but first earnest prayer to God to thrust forth laborers, and secondly the deepening of the spiritual life of the Church, so that men should be unable to stay at home. I saw that the apostolic plan was not to be concerned about ways and means, but to go and do the work, trusting in His sure word who has said, 'Seek ye first the kingdom of God and His righteousness, and all these things shall be added unto you.' "

The more Taylor prayed and studied God's Word and the needs of China, the utter helplessness of its unevangelized people began to weigh as a heavy burden on his mind. A request came to him to write a series of articles for a missionary magazine. As he wrote them he

began to feel how terrible that need was, and how
the Lord's last command was being ignored by His
Church. The careful study of the whole subject brought
out how there were eleven vast interior provinces of
China, each with its tens of millions, without a single
resident Protestant missionary. Gradually the truth
dawned upon him that to undertake the evangelization of
inland China a new and special agency was needed. He
spoke to various representatives of leading missionary
societies, but was met by difficulties, either financial or
political. Their excuses were that the money was lacking,
or that it was not possible to penetrate into the interior
before the country had become more open. He felt how
little the Church had learned to trust the promises of
God. Gradually the thought came, "Well, if you see these
things more clearly than others, why not go forward
yourself, and trust God to accomplish His purposes
through you? Go yourself to inland China. What is to
hinder your obtaining the men and the means?" The
thought raised a controversy in his soul, which gradually
affected his health. The story is told:

'I saw', Taylor says, 'that in answer to prayer
the workers needed would certainly be given, and
their support secured, because it was asked for in
the precious name of Jesus, which is worthy; but
there a trembling unbelief crept in.

'Suppose that workers are given,' I asked
myself doubtfully, 'and that they succeed in
reaching inland China; what then? Trials will
come, and conflicts such as they have never

dreamed of at home. Their faith may fail, and they may even be tempted to reproach me for having brought them into such a plight. Have I strength and ability to cope with such difficulties as these?' And the answer, of course, was always 'No!'

It was just a bringing in of self through unbelief, the devil getting me to feel that while faith and prayer might lead me into the dilemma, I would be left to get out of it as best I might. And I failed to see that the Power that gave the laborers would be quite sufficient also to sustain them, under any circumstances, no matter how trying.

Meanwhile the awful realization was burned into my very soul that, a million a month of the unevangelized in China were dying without God. 'If you would pray for preachers,' came the dread conviction, 'they might have a chance of hearing the glorious gospel; but they are passing away without hearing, simply because you don't have enough faith to claim heralds of the Cross for them.'

Week after week the conflict went on, until the strain became so intense that sleep almost forsook him, and it seemed as if reason itself must fail. Rest was impossible by day or night. The thought of China's millions was always before his mind.

Taylor continues —

How inconsistent unbelief always is! I had

no doubt that in answer to prayer the financial means for our going forth would also be supplied, and that doors would be opened in unreached parts of the Empire. But I had not yet learned to trust God fully for keeping power and grace for myself, so that it was no wonder that I found it difficult to trust Him to keep any others who might be led to go out with me.

Yet what was I to do? The feeling of blood-guiltiness became more and more intense. Simply because I refused to ask for them, the laborers did not come forward, and did not go out to China; and every day tens of thousands in that vast land were living and dying with no knowledge of the way of salvation.

The burden upon his mind began to tell upon Taylor's health. He went down to Brighton, at the invitation of a friend, to take a rest by the sea. When Sunday morning came, hundreds of happy church-goers thronged the streets, but Taylor could only think of the need of the vast land to which his life had been given. "More than a thousand souls in China," he thought, "will be swept into eternity while the people of God, with so many privileges, are gathered in the morning services today!"

In great distress of mind, he left the quiet house and went down to the deserted beach. It was a lovely summer morning; the tide was out and far away upon the silent sands he met the crisis of his life alone with God.

At first there was no light, and the conflict was intense. The only ray of comfort he could obtain was from the strange reflection: "Well, if God, in answer to prayer, does give a band of men for inland China, and they go and reach those distant regions, and they should all die of starvation, they will all go straight to heaven; and if only one Chinese soul is saved, it would be well worth while!" But the thought was agony, for still he could not see that, if God gave the laborers, He would be sure to keep them, even in inland China.

All at once the thought came, "Why should *you* be burdened for this? If you are obeying God, all the responsibility must rest with *Him* and not with you."

What an unspeakable relief!

"Very well," was the immediate, glad reply; "Thou, Lord, shalt be responsible for them, and for me too!" And the burden, from that moment, was all gone.

Then and there Hudson Taylor surrendered himself to God for His service, and lifted up his heart in prayer for fellow-laborers — two for each of the inland provinces, and two for Mongolia. His Bible was in his hand, and there, in the margin of the precious volume, he recorded the momentous transaction that had taken place between his soul and God. Few and simple are the words he uses, but, oh! how full of meaning: "Prayed for twenty-four willing skillful laborers at Brighton, June 25th, 1865.

"How restful I felt when this was done! The conflict was ended. Peace and gladness filled my soul. I felt like flying up the steep hill to the house. And how well I slept that night! My dear wife thought that Brighton had done wonders for me; and so it had!"

I have quoted so much of the story of Hudson Taylor's inner life because it reveals the secret source from which power for true mission work must come. That the unevangelized are fellow-heirs and fellow-members of the body and fellow-partakers of the promise in Christ Jesus through the gospel is a great spiritual mystery, which in other generations was not made known unto the sons of men as it hath now been revealed unto His holy apostles and prophets in the Spirit. Any man can understand the missionary command as Scripture sets it forth, but it requires a spiritual mind to apprehend its true spiritual meaning and power. What Paul writes is as true now as then: "The mystery hath now been manifested to His saints, to whom God was pleased to make known what are the riches of the glory of this mystery among the Gentiles." It needs divine teaching, it needs the revelation of the Holy Spirit, to give a true understanding of the mystery of God.

Hudson Taylor's experience shows us how God trains a man to believe in Him, to wait on Him, to give himself up entirely to His will and service, however great the difficulty may be. The Church needs to learn the lesson, our missionary meetings and our mission sermons must aim at teaching that, as individuals give themselves wholly to God, He will equip them for being used in the service of His kingdom. It was a solemn thing for the Son of God to come to save the world: He had to bear its sins and to die for it. It is equally a solemn thing for us to take part in the work of soul-winning; it requires that we, in faith and love, have a burden for souls, and, if necessary, give our lives for their salvation. And it requires close communion with God, and a full surrender to His guidance, to fit us to do His work.

One more illustration is given of the way in which Taylor sought, in his meetings, to bring Christians into personal contact with God. The first party of twenty-two, including children, was ready to go to China, when the following incident occurred:

I was asked to give a lecture on China at Totteridge, a village near London, and willingly consented to do so, on condition that there should be no collection, and that this should be announced on the publicity. Mr. Puget, who invited me, and presided as chairman, said he had never heard of such a stipulation. He accepted it, however, and the meeting was scheduled.

With the aid of a large map, something of the extent, population, and deep spiritual need of China was presented to the people, many of whom were deeply impressed. At the close of the meeting the chairman said that at my request there had been no collection, but he felt there were many present who would be distressed and burdened if not allowed to contribute something to the good work proposed. He trusted that as this suggestion emanated entirely from himself, and expressed the feelings of the audience, I should not object to it. I begged, however, that the condition agreed upon should not be altered, pointing out that the very reason given by the chairman was, to my mind, one of the strongest for not making any collection.

"My desire was not that those present might be relieved by giving then and there such contributions as might be convenient under the influence of present emotion, but that each one should go home really burdened with a sense of China's deep need, and then ask God what He would have them do. If, after thought and prayer, they were satisfied that a financial contribution was all He wanted of them, this could be given to any society having missionaries at work in China, or could be mailed to our London address. But perhaps in many cases what God was asking was not a money contribution, but personal consecration to His service abroad, or the gift of a dear son or daughter, more precious than gold.

I added that I thought the tendency to take a collection was to leave upon the mind the impression that the all-important thing was money, whereas no amount of money could convert a single soul. The supreme need was that men and women filled with the Holy Spirit should give themselves to the work, and for the support of such there would never be a lack of funds. As my wish was evidently strong, the chairman kindly yielded, and closed the meeting. However, at the supper table He told me that he thought I was sadly mistaken, and that some contributions had been put into his hand for the mission.

Next morning at breakfast my kind host came in a little late, and said he had passed a restless night. After the meal was over he asked me into his study, and, handing me the contributions of the previous evening, remarked: 'I thought yesterday, Mr. Taylor, that you were wrong about the collection, but now I am convinced you are right. As I considered in the night that stream of souls in China, ever passing onward into the dark, I could only cry, as you suggested, "Lord, what wilt Thou have me to do?" I believe I have obtained the guidance I sought; and here it is.' He handed me a check for five hundred pounds, adding that if there had been a collection he would have given a few guineas towards it, but that this check was the result of having spent a greater part of the night in prayer.

I need scarcely say how surprised and thankful I was for the gift. A letter had reached me at the breakfast table that very morning from the shipping agents, in which they stated that they could offer us the whole passenger accommodation of the ship *Lammermuir*. I went, on my way home, to see the ship, found it every way suitable, and paid that check on account. Thus did the Lord encourage our hearts in Himself.*

*These extracts are taken from The Story of the China Inland Mission, by M. Geraldine Guinness, 2 vols.

We are studying the missionary problem. We are seeking the answer to its most important question — *How can the Church be spiritually quickened to do the work with its whole heart, in the power which God can give?* We have been trying to learn from those whom God has specially used and blessed what the secret of their strength is. God had set forth Hudson Taylor as an example of what He can do for a young man who gives himself wholly to live by faith in God as he seeks to do God's work. We have learned that the missionary problem is a personal one. Hudson Taylor's training for fellowship with God was an intensely personal one. Since the missionary problem — how to win the world for God — is only to be solved by each believer giving himself personally to the work, we may learn from this servant of God.

It is easy to say that the answer consists in the prevailing prayer of faith. But how can every believer be trained for this? The lesson is very clear. We have seen the path in which the power of believing prayer came to him. He gave himself wholly to God's work; this gave him the confidence that God would care for him and all his work. Faith cannot grow strong except by exercise. Difficulties are the proving ground of faith; they give it nourishment and strength. A believer who does not realize the difficulty of mission work, because he is not intensely interested in it, cannot taste the privilege of believing, persevering, prevailing prayer. We want to train every believer to take such an interest in the progress of the work of God's kingdom that he may feel and hear the burden of its great need. Only thus can he realize the impossibility of its being done without God's own power, and he may learn to cry for more men and money, for the Spirit's power, and for the ingathering of souls.

Strong desire, personal interest and effort, faith in God's power of working in answer to our prayer: these are the conditions of that prevailing prayer in which every believer can have a share. We need, in our missionary meetings and sermons, to aim at cultivating this. We need to encourage the most insignificant believer to know that he can do much for God's cause. The poor widow did more than she knew by the devotion which her gift mainfested. Let our mission work not only rest on the amount of the gifts we receive, but on the spirit of devotion which offers believing prayer with them. Let it be seen, in our ministers and leaders, in our Churches and societies, that faith in God's working, and continual prayer to secure that working, is the chief element in our hopes. Then and only then will the Church become what she should be, and God will say to her, "Believest thou? Thou shalt see greater things than these."

6

The Church of Pentecost
and the Holy Spirit

We have looked at three cases in which we have seen
how wonderfully God had led His servants in the past
century or so into the secret of power and blessing on the
mission field. Let us now go back to Pentecost, to the
birth of the Christian Church. There are revealed the
great root-principles in which, through all ages, the
Church will find the law of its service and its triumph over
the powers of darkness.

If we take as a basic premise that it is possible to
evangelize the world in this generation — in view of the
achievements of the Christians of the first generation —
then it is a terrible condemnation of the Church of our
day. If we are to gain anything by admitting this, we need
to explore the difference between us and the early
Church. How can we truly walk in their footsteps and do
our work as they did?

Our ascended Lord has not only given us His Holy Spirit, but the men in whom He first came to dwell as living demonstrations of what He is able to do for us too. People are not interested so much in abstract ideas, as in individuals who represent the ideas. The Church of the first generation is given to us by God as an example and a pledge of what the Holy Spirit can do in men who are wholly possessed by Him. If the Church of our day is really to be and to do what God desires, pastors and congregations must be led to study the pentecostal pattern. We should be content with nothing less than an equal devotion to the work of making Christ known everywhere. A tree can only grow strong by abiding in the root from which it was born. The missionary revival which we need and pray for within the Church, before she is fitted to do her work, can only come by a return to Pentecost. The end is ever contained in the beginning, and returns to the beginning. The only power to evangelize the world in this generation, lies in knowing what Pentecost means and to have its faith and its Spirit.

The great commission was given in connection with Pentecost, and its fulfillment was made entirely dependent on it. "And that repentance and remission of sins should be preached in his name among all nations, beginning at Jerusalem. And ye are witnesses of these things. And, behold, I send the promise of my Father upon you: but tarry ye in the city of Jerusalem, until ye be endued with power from on high." (Luke 24:47-49) "But ye shall receive power, after that the Holy Ghost is come upon you: and ye shall be witnesses unto me both in

Jerusalem, and in all Judaea, and in Samaria, and unto the uttermost part of the earth." (Acts 1:8) *The pentecostal commission can only be carried out by a pentecostal Church, in pentecostal power.* The charge has been laid against the Church of our day, and admitted, that she is not what she ought to be. How can we think of this generation accomplishing the pentecostal commission without a return to the pentecostal state? The great burning question of the missionary problem is, how can the Church be brought back to the place where the discipline and the early Church were, when, in the power of the Holy Spirit, they did what no other generation since has done? The Church of Pentecost was not merely an example and pledge of what God could do, leaving it to us to choose if we would enjoy the same blessing. No, it is much more — a revelation of God's will as to what His Church ought to be, and of what is absolutely indispensable if there is to be any real hope of securing obedience to the great commission. The pentecostal state is the only one that satisfies God, the only one that ought to satisfy us.

Like all seed, Pentecost was a fruit too: The fruit not only of Christ's work for us on the cross and in heaven, but the fruit also of His work in the disciples in preparing them to receive the Spirit. The pastor needs to learn what the missionary enthusiasm of his ministry ought to be, and how he can communicate it to his people; the leader of a mission group wants to find for his circle the full equipment for the service of the kingdom; every believer desires to personally learn from his Lord the secret of entire devotion to His work, of being filled with His Spirit, and of winning souls to the knowledge of His love. To accomplish this, we must become learners in the school in which Christ trained His disciples. There we find how after Christ went to heaven they were equipped to be the vessels and channels of the Spirit on earth.

The first coming of the Holy Spirit in power was to a prepared people. For the Church in our day to receive the Spirit in pentecostal power, we need the same preparation. This involves giving up and forsaking all that hinders, an emptying and a cleansing of ourselves and a thirsting, waiting and entire surrender to Christ. Then the blessing of the Spirit's power surely comes.

What were the chief elements of that training? There was, first of all, a calling out and separation from the ordinary interests and claims of daily life. The principle that underlies the life of all God's great servants in the previous ages — Abraham and Joseph, Moses and Joshua, David and Elijah — is taking them out of and setting them apart from their ordinary environment. Often this happened through persecution and suffering, that they might be brought into solitude with God alone, and be released from what is otherwise innocent or lawful on earth. Thus free, they can listen to the Divine voice, receive the Divine revelation, be changed and fitted by the Divine power for their work. Even so Christ called His disciples to forsake all, to deny themselves of what others might consider perfectly legitimate, and to share with Him, His cross and all it may involve. For three years He had them in His training — by dialogue with them, by letting them watch what He did, by His reproofs and instructions. He was preparing them to be the recipients and channels of the Holy Spirit, who would come to take the place of His earthly presence, and open within them His abiding indwelling.

In a sinful world, sacrifice is the law of life and of love. The men whom Christ had fitted to become the leaders of the pentecostal Church, and to embody in their lives the mind and life of the Spirit, learned to give up everything for Christ. As their Lord could not give Himself for them without sacrificing all, they, too, had learned, in giving themselves, to part with all for the sake of His service and kingdom. In that entire self-abandonment to one purpose the pentecostal Church had struck its roots deep.

When there is no persecution, when money, comfort and Christian civilization surround us, when it appears to cost little to be a Christian, many find it difficult to know where the forsaking all to become a disciple comes in, or what shape it will assume. The answer is the second great element in Christ's training of His disciples: They had an intense personal attachment to Christ.

When Christ first called them, there was something in Him that attracted them and made that call irresistible. As Christ drew them without their knowing how and why, so He led them by a way and to a goal they did not know. They began by believing in Him as the Messiah: He led them on to know Him as the Son of God, as Friend, as Master, and Redeemer. Of His love to them, or theirs to Him, He said little or nothing till the last night of His life. Then He opened up to them the mystery of His loving them with a Divine love — of His giving His life for them, of the Father's love resting on them, of their loving Him and keeping His commandments. The disciples had not followed Him with any such aim; it was Christ who had, by His Divine love, in the course of His three years' training, attached them to Himself. It is this intense personal living attachment to Christ that prepares us for receiving the Holy Spirit, and brings us that pentecostal power without which the Church cannot hope to conquer the world.

Detachment comes only through a new and stronger attachment. As a Christian sees that, though he knows so little of his Lord's love, the Lord is ready to lead him on to it in a way he does not know. He becomes willing to turn away from everything that can occupy the heart, and to yield himself, in patient obedient discipleship, to the influences of his relationship with his Lord. He learns to know that that love can master him. The love of Christ asks and claims the whole heart and life. If we are really to appeal to our churches to follow in the footsteps of the pentecostal Church, and to claim her power and blessing, we must encourage them to enter the school in which Christ trained His disciples. When the love of Christ becomes everything to any of us, and we yield ourselves to His love, demonstrated in dying for sinners, that love will teach us, it will constrain us, to part with all for this pearl of great price. Detachment from the world, attachment to Christ, are the secrets of pentecostal blessing.

Closely connected with this love, as another element of preparation for Pentecost, was the brotherly love which Christ had taught them. He not only bound them to Himself, but also to each other. Christ always dealt with individuals. He calls His sheep by name. He knows and meets the needs of each. But His work does not end there. He makes each one a member of His body. The Divine life is a life of love. He leads us into a life of love; He calls us and His Spirit enables us to love each other as He loved us. His own love dwells in us, and binds the body into a living whole. This supernatural and divine love is to be the Church's power to convince the world of her Divine origin. The union this love gives brings strength to each member, multiplying the strength of all by the aid derived from the whole body. It was this love that often made men say, "See how they love one another." It was this love, in the unity of the body, that made weak men and women strong to conquer.

This love was cultivated in close fellowship, both in Christ's lifetime and after the Spirit came. It is this fellowship of love that is often sadly lacking in a congregation or a society. A hundred men contribute to the same collection for mission work, and partake of the same Holy Supper, and yet know nothing of the interchange of mutual love and spiritual fellowship. When we begin to seek Christ's Spirit in earnest for our mission work, or when we think that His first movings are felt, let us remember that there is no place where the Spirit works so surely as when we are gathered together with our brothers in the Name of Jesus. To speak together of that name and love has more to do with our spiritual life than we think. To give ourselves to encourage the weak, to instruct the ignorant, to warn the erring, by telling what Christ is to us, is one of the surest means of drawing down the presence of the Lord. This builds the separate members into one body, rouses the hope of all and prepares them for that blessed outpouring of the Spirit which is indispensable if we are to witness for Christ in power.

Faith was one of the chief lessons needed for the pentecostal mission work of the first century and of ours. Christ directly taught His disciples about faith; then indirectly He talked about it in their hearing, he proved the indispensability of faith in their presence, He instructed them as to the conditions and the power of faith. More than that, He impressed upon them the place faith must have in their life and work.

We know what faith is. From the first simple faith that hears a promise and believes God's Word, to the faith that enters into full and conscious union with our Lord, and abides in Him and does the "greater works," faith is always one of the first conditions of the power of the Spirit's working. The pentecostal Church received and maintained her blessing and power, did her work, endured her sufferings, and triumphed — all through faith.

Faith is such a simple thing that many think it an easy thing. As the power to overcome the world, and cast out Satan, and bring men out of darkness into God's light, it is no easy thing. It implies renunciation of self, crucifixion to the world, ceasing from the wisdom and power of man, and depending on God alone. We speak of faith missions, in which faith, in some of its special aspects is especially prominent. We need to emphasize the real truth that *all mission work is to be faith work.* If this is to be so, we must begin at the beginning, and seek not only to have the Word mixed with faith in them that hear, but to have all our work and prayer mixed with faith too. "By faith Abel offered unto God a more excellent sacrifice than Cain . . ." (Heb. 11:4)

When the offering of money in a collection is as sacred a thing as the offering of prayer, when the faith which is essential to make a prayer effectual, we shall find the point of contact in dealing with individual believers. Only then will our missionary meetings and collections become as helpful to the life of faith as the preaching of the gospel. When individuals grasp this reality, so will the various societies and congregations to which they belong. Then, with the leaders and directors and missionaries, all should unite in the one deep and overmastering conviction: *Misson work is faith work.* When all our workers at home and abroad acknowledge that this faith is indispensable — because they know personally Christ's power to save and triumph and work in them — we shall be approaching a new pentecostal era.

When Christ ascended to the throne, was the preparation complete? Not yet. One more thing was needed to finish the work. Even after the disciples had been trained by Jesus for three years, after they felt the mysterious influence of His death, and were breathed into by the mighty power of His resurrection life; although they had the wonderful revelations of His new life for forty days, and watched Him ascend from the earth to Heaven — they still needed something. *It was the ten days of continued, united prayer and supplication.* I hardly know a passage in Scripture which presents prayer in such a wondrous light. God had done all that was needed; Christ had finished His work for His disciples and in them; but Pentecost still had to wait ten days for their prayers. Prayer put the finishing touch to the work of preparation. Prayer expresses a complete and continuous turning away from earth, and arising into heaven, an opening of the whole being to God, and abiding in Christ. Such prayer proved that those men were indeed prepared vessels for God's Holy Spirit.

When Jesus the Lamb had been glorified and had taken His place in the midst of the throne, the river of the water of life broke forth from the throne of God and the Lamb. It flowed as streams of living water into and out of these praying disciples. Christ was the pattern: "And it came to pass that, Jesus also being baptized, and praying, the heaven was opened, and the Holy Ghost descended upon Him." (Luke 3:21, 22) When every other condition has been fulfilled, continued prayer is needed to bring down the blessing. If the pentecostal Church is an example, and it cannot be without the pentecostal era being repeated, prayer must again be the key that opens the windows of heaven. Prayer must be preached and practiced as the first and the last duty of a church that hopes to have the power of God seen in its work. The ten days' continued prayer teaches a simple lesson yet so difficult to master, that what *little* prayer does not obtain, *much* earnest believing prayer, continued long enough, will bring down.

We have said that the early church availed herself of no power which we cannot utilize. We have seen what some of these powers are. The power of separation from the world and true self-sacrifice, of intense attachment and devotion to Jesus, of love and fellowship making us one with the saints around us, of faith, and of continued prayer. These things made the disciples ready to receive the promise of the Father, and be the fit instruments for the Holy Spirit's mighty work in witnessing for Christ to the uttermost parts of the earth.

Men are wonderfully formed to have, in human nature, as Jesus had, the Spirit of God dwelling in them. How wonderful this blessing was in itself — the fruit and the crown of Christ's redeeming work. These men, prepared by Christ, were all filled with the Holy Spirit. On earth Christ's body had been the home of the Spirit and the instrument of His work. Mortal men are now His body; they take His place; the Spirit dwells in them as the instruments for and the continuance of Christ's own work. The Spirit, through whom God is God, and Father and Son, each is what He is, and both are One — that Spirit, the very life of God, fills them.

In the threefold operation of His quickening grace, He enlightens, He sanctifies, He strengthens. That is, He reveals divine truth, He makes us partakers of the holy life and disposition of Christ, and He endues us with the divine power that, in the midst of weakness, triumphs through us. As Christ's training was to prepare them, so this enduement was actually to fit them for His work. "Ye shall receive power when the Holy Ghost is come upon you." God's power for God's work was to be the one condition of success in their undertaking to bring the gospel to the ends of the earth.

That pentecostal generation did more to accomplish the evangelization of the world than any succeeding generation. Considering the increase in the population of the world and the increase of the Church, we ought to do tenfold more than they did. But even if we are to do *as much as* they did, we need this one thing: *To be filled with the Holy Spirit, as the Power of God, to do the work of God!* It is not enough that the river of the water of life is still flowing from under the throne of God and the Lamb; it is not enough that we are the temple of God, and the Spirit of God dwells in us. The Spirit may be in us, and yet be grieved, or quenched, or resisted, or neglected. Where He is to work in power, He asks to fill the whole being. He claims control of the whole life. We are to be led and ruled by Him in everything. He asks that the man shall be a living sacrifice, a whole burnt-offering, to be consumed by the fire of God.

If there is to be any hope of our working like the Church of Pentecost, we must have a new era in our missions. There must be a real restoration of the pentecostal life and power in the Church at home. *The power of God for the work of God* must be the watchword of every worker. Only then will our mission work, both in its extent and its intensity, be able to reach those who are still without the knowledge of Christ. If we are to take the foregoing seriously, what are we to do about it? We must confess that the overwhelming majority of our Church members are very far from Pentecost. *What is to be done to get all our leaders in churches and boards, in societies and committees, to take up the watchword: Back to Pentecost: without this the work cannot be done.* We must gather our pastors, congregation and all who feel that God's work is not being done as it should be, into one holy bond of union until the watchword has echoed through the Church: *Back to Pentecost: God's power for God's work; without this the work cannot be done.*

The missionary problem is a personal one. Every believer, in receiving the love of Christ into his heart, has taken in a love that reaches out to the whole world. The great commission rests on every member of the Church. Let each of us begin with himself in seeking for the Church the restoration of her pentecostal power for the work of conquering the world for her King.

It was prayer that brought Pentecost — intense, continued, united prayer. That prayer did not cease until it was answered. Such prayer is not an easy thing.

Hudson Taylor said at the Conference: "Not only must missionaries suffer in going forth, but the Church must go forward in self-denial to the point of suffering. Redemptive work, soul-saving work, cannot be carried on without suffering. If we are simply to pray as a pleasant, and enjoyable exercise, and know nothing of watching in prayer, and weariness in prayer, we shall not draw down the available blessing. We shall not sustain our missionaries, who are overwhelmed with the appalling darkness of heathenism; we shall not even sufficiently maintain the spiritual life of our own souls. We must serve God even to the point of suffering; each one must ask himself, 'To what degree, at what point, am I extending, by personal suffering, by personal self-denial even to the point of pain, the kingdom of Christ?"

Let us give ourselves anew to prayer, that the church may be restored to her pentecostal state. Let us by faith yield ourselves wholly to the Spirit, and receive Him by faith to fill us. Let us give ourselves to prayer for the power of the Spirit in the life and work of the Church at home and abroad. The pentecostal command to preach the gospel to every creature is urgent, all the more from having been neglected so long. Prayer brought Pentecost. Prayer still brings it. But few feel how weak our power in prayer is.

What was it that started those humble fishermen and women praying like that? It was this one thing: Jesus Christ had their whole heart. They had forsaken everything for Him. His love filled them and made them one with Him, and with each other. The fellowship of love strengthened them. Their ascended Lord was everything to them; they couldn't help praying. Let us pray in secret. Let us unite in love with others, and pray without ceasing, and watch unto prayer that, for the sake of His Son and a perishing world, God will restore His people to their first estate in the devotion and power and joy of Pentecost.

Let us always remember: The missionary problem is a personal one. A passionate love to Jesus Christ, born out of His love, truly possessing each of us personally, will teach us to pray, to labor, and to suffer. *Let us pray for such a love.*

7

The Missionary Problem is a Personal One

In a report of the Students' Missionary Conference held in London in January 1900, the Appendix showed a diagram under the heading, THE POSSIBILITIES OF PERSONAL WORK. The statement followed: "IF there were only one Christian in the world, and he worked and prayed a year to win one friend to Christ, and IF these two then continued each year to win one more, and IF every person thus led into the kingdom led another to Christ every year, in thirty-one years every person in the world would be won for Christ." The mathematical progression showed that at the end of the thirty-one years there would be over two billion Christians.

Some may doubt the validity of calculations which lie altogether beyond the range of possibility or the promises of God's Word. Others may question the correctness of a calculation which appears to count upon all who become

Christians living for thirty-one years, while we know that something like one-thirtieth of the earth's population dies each year. Leaving such questions aside, I wish simply to take the principle which forms the basis of the calculation. I wish to point out what the effect would be if the substantial truth it contains were really believed and preached, and practiced. That truth is this: *Christ meant every believer to be a soul-winner.* Or rather, for this is the deeper truth in which the former has its root and strength, that every believer has been saved with the express purpose that he should make the saving of other souls the main, the supreme end of his existence in the world.

If ever I feel the need of the teaching of the Holy Spirit for myself and my readers it is when I come to this point. We so easily accept general statements without realizing fully what they imply. It is only when we are brought face to face with them, and challenged to apply and act upon them, that the secret unbelief comes out that robs them of their power. Only by the Holy Spirit can we look beyond the present state of the Church and the great majority of Christians, and realize what actually is the will of our God concerning His people, and what He has actually made possible to them in the grace of His Holy Spirit. When we teach the Church our motto must be: *Every believer a soul-winner!* This alone will give a sure foundation for our missionary appeal, and our hope for an immediate and a sufficient response to the call to make Christ known to every person.

But is this statement, *every believer a soul-winner,* literally true and binding? Is it not something impractical? Something beyond the reach of the majority of true but weak believers? The very fact that this truth seems strange to so many and so difficult for any but the spiritual mind to grasp as possible and obligatory, is the most urgent reason to teach it. Let us see the grounds on which it rests.

Nature teaches us that it must be so: It is an essential part of the new nature. We see it in every child who loves to tell of his happiness and to bring others to share his joys. We expect to find in every human heart a feeling of compassion for the poor and the suffering. So why should it be thought strange that every child of God is called to take part in making known the happiness he has found, to concern himself about those who are perishing, to have compassion on them, and work for their salvation? *Every believer a soul-winner!* What can be more natural?

Christ called His disciples the light of the world. The believer is an intelligent being — his light does not shine as a blind force of nature, but is the voluntary reaching out of his heart towards those who are in darkness. He longs to bring the light to them, to do all he can do to make them acquainted with Christ Jesus. The light is often used to illustrate the silent influence which good works and a consistent life may have. Yes, this is an essential element, but it means a great deal more. It does not mean, as is often thought, that I am to be content with finding my own salvation, and trusting that my example will do others good. No! Even as Christ's example derived its power from the fact that it was a life lived for us and given up on our behalf, so the true power of the Christian's influence lies in the love that gives itself away in seeking the happiness of others. As God is light and love, it is love that makes the Christian the light of the world. *Every believer a soul-winner* — this is indeed the law of the Spirit of life in Christ Jesus.

How could it be otherwise? As God is love, so is he that loveth born of God. Love is God's highest glory, His everlasting blessedness. God's children bear His image, share His blessedness, and are the heirs of His glory. But this cannot be in any other way than by their living a life of love. The new life in them is a life of love; how can it manifest itself but in loving as God loves, in loving those whom God loves? It is God's own love that is shed abroad in our hearts. Christ prayed "that the love wherewith Thou lovest Me may be in them." It is the love of Christ, the love with which He loved us, that constrains us. Love cannot change its nature when it flows down from God into us: it still loves the evil ones and the unworthy. Christ's love has no way, now that He is in heaven, of reaching the souls for whom He died, for whom He longs, but through us. Surely nothing can be more natural and true than the blessed message: *Every believer redeemed to be a soul-winner*.

But why, if it is so simple and so sure, are so many words needed to prove and enforce it? Alas! Because the Church is in a weak and sickly state, and tens of thousands of its members have never learned that this is one of the choicest treasures of their heritage. They are content with the selfish thought of personal salvation, and even in the struggle for holiness never learn the Divine purpose for their salvation. And there are tens of thousands more who have some thought of its being part of their calling, yet who have looked upon it as a command beyond their strength. They have never known that, as a law and a power of their inmost nature, its fulfilment is meant to be a normal function of a healthy body in joy and strength.

Even the commandments of our Lord Jesus may be to us as great a burden as the law of Moses, bringing bondage and condemnation, unless we know the twofold secret that brings the power of performance. That secret is first what we have already named — the faith that *love is the inward law of our new nature,* and that the Spirit of God's law is within us to enable us gladly to love, and bless, and save those around us. Second, that it is in the *surrender to a life of close following* and continual fellowship with the Lord Jesus — rejoicing in Him, forsaking all for Him, yielding all to the service of His love — that our spiritual nature can be strengthened. Then the work of winning souls becomes the highest joy and fulfillment of the Christian life. To those who in some measure understand this, there is nothing strange in the thought: *Every believer a soul-winner!* This ought to be the theme of every pastor's preaching and every believer's life.

But even this is not all. Many will agree that every believer is called upon to live and work for others, but still looks upon this as only a secondary thing, additional and subordinate to the primary interest of working out his own salvation. *Every believer a soul-winner* — that does not mean, *among other things,* but *first of all,* as the chief reason of his existence. We all agree in saying that the one and supreme end of the Church is to bring the world to Christ. We know that God gave Him the Church as His body. The one purpose was that it should be to its Head what every body is on earth — the living organ or instrument through which the purposes and the work of the head can be carried out. What is true of the Head, is true of the Body; what is true of the Body, is true of each individual member — even the very weakest. As in the Head, Christ Jesus, as in the Body, the Church, so in every believer, the supreme, the sole end of our being is the saving of souls. It is in this, above everything, that God is glorified. "I have chosen you, and ordained you, that ye should go and should bring forth fruit."

Many may be brought to agree to this truth and yet have to confess that they do not feel its full force. Many a minister may feel how little he is able to preach it, compared with the full conviction with which he preaches grace for salvation. It is well that we should give such confessions careful consideration. Where does the difficulty come in? This union with the Lord Jesus, to participate in His saving work to such an extent that without us He cannot do it, that through us He will and can accomplish it in Divine power, is a deep spiritual mystery. It is an honor altogether too great for us to understand. It is a fellowship and union and partnership so intimate and Divine that the Holy Spirit alone must reveal it to us.

To simple, childlike souls the reality of it comes without their knowing how. Some have lived long in the Christian life and lost the first love, and to them everything has to come by the slow way of the understanding. Such people need humility to give up preconceived opinions, and the confidence of being able to grasp spiritual truths. They also need patient waiting for the Spirit to work such truth in their inmost parts. Above all, we need to turn away from the world, with its spirit and wisdom, and return to closer fellowship with Jesus Christ, from whom alone come light and love. *Every believer ordained to be first and foremost a soul-winner.* Simple though it sounds, it will cost much to many before it has mastered them.

We are often at a loss to understand the need of much continued communion with God. And yet it is the same as with the things of earth. Take the gold put into the furnace. Exposed to insufficient heat, it gets heated but not melted. Exposed to an intense heat for only a short time, and then taken out again, it is not melted. It needs an intense and continuous heat, before the precious but hard metal is prepared for the goldsmith's work. So it is with the fire of God's love. They who would know it in its power, and in power to proclaim and convey it to others, must keep in contact with the love of Christ. They must know it in its intensity, and know what it is to continue in it till their whole being realizes that that love can reach all, and melt all. It can make even the coldest and weakest child of God a lover and seeker of souls. In that intense and continuous fire a pastor, a leader, can learn to witness in power to the truth — *Every believer a soul-winner.*

Let us consider again the illustration of the head and the body. The lessons are so obvious. The head can do nothing but through the body. Each member is as completely under the control of the head as the whole body. If the members, owing to disease, refuse to act, the head is helpless to carry out its plans. The object of the head is, first, to use every member for the preservation and welfare of the whole body, and then to let it take its share in the work the body has to do. If our being members of Christ's Body has any meaning — and praise God it has an infinite meaning — every believer is in the Body to care for the other members, and all to co-operate with the others in working out the plans of the Head. Wherever I go, whatever I do, I carry every member of my body with me, and they take part in all I do.

It is the same in the Body of Christ Jesus. Every member has only one objective and, while healthy, is every moment fulfilling that objective — to carry out the work of the Head. The work of our Head in heaven is to gather all the members of His Body on earth. In this work every member of the body co-operates; not under the law of a blind force of nature, but under the law of the Spirit of life, which connects every believer with his Lord in love, and imparts to him the same disposition and the same strength in which Christ does His work. Each time we read of Christ the Head, and His Body the Church, let us with new emphasis pronounce the motto — *Every member, like Christ, a soul-winner.*

What has this to do with out missionary discussion? We seek to make it the keynote of this book — *The missionary problem is a personal one.* If the Church is really to take up its work, it is not enough that we speak of the obligation resting upon the present generation to make Christ known to everyone. True education must always deal with the individual mind. To the general command must always be added the personal one. Nelson's signal, "England expects every man to do his duty," was a personal appeal addressed to every seaman, not just his fleet. As we seek to find out why, with such millions of Christians, the real army of God that is fighting the hosts of darkness is so small, the only answer is — lack of heart. The enthusiasm of the kingdom is missing. And that is because there is so little enthusiasm for *the King.* Though much may be done by careful organization and strict discipline and good generalship to make the best of the few troops we have, there is nothing that can so restore confidence and courage as the actual presence of a beloved King, to whom every heart beats warm in loyalty and devotion.

The missionary appeal must go deeper and seek to deal with the very root of the evil. If there is no desire for soul-winning at home, how can the interest in the distant unevangelized be truly deep or spiritual? There may be many motives to which we appeal effectively in asking for supplies of men and money — the compassion of a common humanity, the alleviation of the evils of pagan people, the elevation of fellow-human beings in the scale of human life, the claims of our church or society. But the true and highest motive is the only one that will really call forth the spiritual power of the Church, for the work to be done.

If the missionary appeal to this generation to bring the gospel to every person is to be successful, the Church will have to gird itself for the work in a very different way from what it has been doing. The most serious question the Church has to face just now — in fact, the only real difficulty of the missionary problem — is how she is to be awakened as a whole to the greatness and glory of the task entrusted to her and led to engage in it with all her heart and strength. The only answer to that question — the key to the whole situation — appears to be the simple truth: *The missionary problem is a personal one.* The Lord Jesus Christ is the Author and Leader of Missions. Whoever stands right with Him, and abides in Him, will be ready to know and do His will. It is simply a matter of *being near enough to Him to hear His voice, and so devoted to Him and His love as to be ready to do all His will.* Christ's whole relation to each of us is an intensely personal one. He loved *me* and gave Himself for *me.* My relation to Him is an entirely personal one. He gave Himself a ransom for me, and I am His, to live for *Him* and *His* glory. He has breathed His love into my heart, and I love Him. He tells me that, as a member of His Body, He needs me for His service, and in love I gladly yield myself to Him. He wants nothing more than that I should tell this to others, prove to them how He loves, how He enables us to love, and how blessed is a life in His love.

The personal element of the missionary problem must be put in the foreground. Every missionary sermon or meeting must give the love of Christ the first place. If Christians are in a low, cold, worldly state, the first object must be to wait on God in prayer and faith for His Holy Spirit to lead them to a true devotion to Jesus Christ. Will that be an apparent loss of time in not beginning at once with the ordinary missionary information and pleas? Ah, no — it will soon be made up. Weak believers, who are glad to hear and give, must be lifted to the consciousness of the wonderful spiritual privilege of offering *themselves* to Christ to live for His kingdom. They must be encouraged to believe that the Lord who loves them, greatly prizes their love, and will enable them to bring it to Him. They must learn that Christ's dying love asks for whole-hearted devotion, and that the more they sacrifice, the more will that love possess them. As definitely as we labor to secure the interest and the gifts of each individual, even more so must we labor to bring each one into contact with Christ Himself.

At first it may appear as if we are aiming too high. In many congregations the response may be very weak. Let the pastor give himself to study the missionary problem in this light. Let him put it to his people, clearly and perseveringly: You have been redeemed to be the witnesses and messengers of Christ's love. To fit you for it, His love has been given you, and shed abroad in your heart. As He loves you, He loves the whole world. He wants those who know it to tell those who don't know it. His love to you and to them, your love to Him and to them, call you to do it. It is your highest privilege; it will be your highest happiness and perfection. As Christ gave Himself, *give yourself* wholly to this work of love.

8

The Responsibility of Leadership in Missions

In the opening chapter a number of quotations were given in which the chief responsibility for the solution of the missionary problem was, by common consent, laid upon the Christian leadership. *To the pastor belongs the privilege and responsibility of the foreign missionary problem.* These words, apparently endorsed by the whole conference, point, in connection with the ministry, to a high honor, a serious shortcoming, an urgent duty, and the great need of seeking from God the grace to worthily fulfill its vocation. We don't need to seek to apportion exactly the measure of responsibility between the ministry and the membership of the Church. That a holy and heavy responsibility rests on the ministry in this matter, all agree. Let all ministers heartily admit and accept it, and prepare themselves to live up to it.

What is the ground on which that responsibility rests? The principles out of which it grows are simple, and yet of inconceivable importance. They are these four: That *missions are the chief end of the Church.* That *the chief end of the ministry is to guide the Church in this work, and equip her for it.* That *the chief end of the preaching to a congregation ought to be to train it to help to fulfill her destiny.* And that *the chief end of every minister in this connection ought to be to fit himself thoroughly for this work.*

Let no one think these statements are exaggerated. They may appear to be because we have been so accustomed to give missions a very subordinate place in our Church and her ministry. We need to be brought back to the great central truth, "the mystery of God," that the Church is the Body of Christ, absolutely and exclusively ordained by God to carry out the purpose of His redeeming love in the world. Even as Christ, the Church has only one objective, to be the light of the world. As Christ died for every man, as God wills that all men should be saved, so the Spirit of God in the Church knows only this purpose — that the gospel should be brought to every creature. *Missions are the chief end of the Church.* All the work of the Holy Spirit in converting sinners and edifying believers, has this for its one aim — to fit them for the part that each must take in winning back the world to God. Nothing else than what God's eternal purpose and Christ's dying love is, can be the goal of the Church.

As we see this to be true, we shall see that *the chief end of the ministry ought to be to equip the Church for this.* Paul writes, "God gave pastors and teachers for the perfecting of the saints unto (what these saints have to do) the work of ministering, or serving, unto (the final aim of this work of the saints) the building up of the body of Christ." (Eph. 4:12) It is through the ministering, the loving service of the saints that the body of Christ is to be gathered and built up. Pastors and teachers are given to perfect the saints for this work of ministering.

A Teachers' College or Training Class is very different from an ordinary school. It seeks not only to train every student to acquire and possess knowledge *for himself,* but to fit him to impart it *to others.* Each congregation is meant to be a training class. Every believer, without exception, is to be "perfected," to be thoroughly prepared for the work of ministering and taking his part in labor and prayer for those near and far. In all the pastor's teaching of repentance and conversion, of obedience and holiness, this ought definitely to be his ultimate aim — to call men to come and serve God in the noble, holy, Christ-like work of saving the lost and restoring God's kingdom on earth. The chief end of the Church is of necessity the chief end of the ministry.

Out of this follows, naturally, the statement that *the chief aim of preaching* ought to be to train every believer and every congregation to take its part in helping the Church fulfill her destiny. This will decide the question as to how often a missionary sermon ought to be preached. As long as only one missionary message a year is given, it is possible that the chief thought will be the obtaining of a better collection. This may often be obtained without the spiritual life being raised at all. When missions take their true place as the chief purpose of the church in which the missionary spirit has really taken possession, a minister may feel the need, time after time, to return to the one subject, until the neglected truth begins to master at least some in the congregation. At times it may be that while there is no direct preaching on missions, yet all the teaching on love and faith, on obedience and service, on holiness and conformity to Christ, may be inspired by this one truth — that we are to be "imitators of God, and walk in love, even as Christ loved us and gave Himself a sacrifice for us."

This now leads up to what, in view of the responsibility of the minister, is the main point — that *the chief aim of every minister* ought to be to equip himself for this great work. To be a teacher in a Teachers' College or Training School needs special training. To inspire and train and help believers is not easy; it does not come from the mere fact that one is an earnest Christian, and has had ministerial training. It is a matter of giving much larger place to missions in our theological seminaries. But even this can only be partial and preparatory. The minister needs to prepare himself to successfully combat the selfishness that is content with personal salvation, the worldliness that has no idea of sacrificing all or even anything for Christ, the unbelief that measures its power to help or bless by what it feels and sees. Without doubt he will need special training to fit him for this, the highest and holiest part of his vocation.

How can the minister prepare himself for carrying out his responsibility? The first answer will usually be, by study. Many pertinent things were said about this at the Conference which are especially applicable to the pastor, as the representative and guide of his people.

Mrs. J. T. Gracey pointed out: "Possibly one of the greatest factors in the development of missionary interest is the systematic study of missions."

How often, in the study of the Bible or theology, everything is simply regarded as a matter of the intellect, leaving the heart unchanged. It is possible for a man to study and know the theory and history of missions, and yet lack the inspiration that knowledge was meant to give. To study science with wonder and reverance and humility is a great gift — how much more is all this needed in the higher area of the spiritual world, and especially in this, the highest destiny of the Church, "the mystery of God"!

To study missions, we need a deep humility that is conscious of its ignorance, and has no confidence in its own understanding; reverant waiting and patience that is willing to listen to what God's Spirit can reveal; and love and devotion that allows itself to be mastered and led by divine love wherever He leads.

And what is it that a pastor will need especially to study? In the missionary problem there are three great factors. The world in its sin and misery; Christ in His dying love; the Church as the link between the two.

The first thing is: Study the world. Take some of the statistics that tell of its population. Think, for instance, of the millions of unevangelized dying every month; dropping over the precipice into the gloom of thick

darkness at the rate of more than one every second. Or
take some book that brings you face to face with the sin
and degradation and suffering of some special country.
Study its diagrams, its maps, its statistics. Stop and ask
yourself whether you believe, whether you *feel,* what you
have read. Pause and meditate and pray, asking God to
give you an eye to see and a heart to feel that misery.
Think of these millions as your fellow human beings.

Look at that picture of a man worshipping a cobra cut
in stone with a reverence of which many Christians know
little. Take in what it means until you cannot forget it.
That man is your brother. He has, like you, a nature
formed for worship. He does not, like you, know the true
God. Will you not sacrifice everything, even yourself, to
save him? Study the state of the world, sometimes in its
great whole, sometimes in its detail, until you begin to feel
that God has placed you in this dark world with the one
object of studying that darkness, and living and helping
those who are dying in it.

If at times you feel that it is more than you can bear,
cry to God to help you to look again, and yet again, until
you know the need of the world. But remember always,
the strongest intellect, the most vivid imagination, the
most earnest study, cannot give you the right
understanding of these things. Nothing but the Spirit and
love of Jesus can make you feel what He feels, and love as
He loves.

Then comes the second great lesson: Christ's love,
dying for these sinners, and now longing to have them
won for Him. Oh, do not think you already know that

dying love, that love resting on and thirsting for every creature on earth! If you would study the missionary problem, study it in the heart of Jesus. The missionary problem is very personal — one that applies to every believer. But it is especially true of the minister, who is to be the pattern and the teacher of believers. Study, experience and prove the power of the personal relationship, so that you may be able to teach well this deepest secret of true mission work.

And then with Christ's love there is His power. Study this until the vision of a triumphant Christ, with every enemy at His feet, has cast its light upon the whole earth. The whole work of saving men is Christ's work, as much today as on Calvary, as much with each individual conversion as in the propitiation for the sins of all. His divine power carries on the work in and through His servants. In studying the possible solution of the problem, in any case of special difficulty, beware of leaving out the omnipotence of Jesus. Humbly, reverently and patiently worship Him, until Christ's love and power become the inspiration of your life.

The third great lesson to study is — the Church, the connecting link between the dying Saviour and the dying world. Here some of the deepest mysteries of the missionary problem will be found: That the Church should really be the Body of Christ on earth, with the Head in heaven, as indispensable to Him as He is to it! That His omnipotence and His infinite redeeming love should have linked themselves, for the fulfillment of His desires, to the weakness of His Church! That the Church should now these many years have heard the declaration, *Missions the Supreme end of the Church,* and yet be content with such a poor achievement! That the Lord should yet be waiting to prove most wonderfully how really He counts His Church one with Himself, and is ready to fill her with His Spirit, power and glory! That there is abundant ground for a confident faith that the Lord is able and waiting to restore the Church to her pentecostal state, and so fit her for carrying out her pentecostal commission!

In the midst of such study there will grow the clearer conviction of how actually the Church is His Body, endued with the power of His Spirit, true partaker of His Divine love, the blessed partner of His life and His glory. Such faith will be awakened if the Church will arise and give herself wholly to her Lord. *The pentecostal glory can still return.*

The world in its sin and woe, Christ in His love and power, the Church as the link between the two — these are the three great magnitudes the minister must know if he is to master the missionary problem. In his study he may go to Scripture, to missionary literature, and to books on theology or the spiritual life; but in the long run he will always have to come back to the truth: the problem is a personal one. It demands a complete and unreserved giving up of the whole being to live for that world, for that Christ, for that Church. The living Christ can manifest Himself through us; He can impart His love in power. He can make His love ours, so that we may feel as He does. He can let the light of His love fall on the world, to reveal its need and its hope. He can give the experience of how close and how real His union is with the believer, and how divinely He can dwell and work in us.

The missionary problem is a personal one, to be solved by the power of Christ's love. The minister must study it, so he will learn to preach in new power—missions, the great work, the supreme end, of Christ, of the Church, of every congregation, of every believer, and especially of every minister.

We have said that the first need of the ministry, if it is to fulfill its calling to missions, is to study them. But when light begins to come, and the mind is convinced and the emotions are stirred, these must immediately be translated into action, if they are not to remain barren. And where shall this action begin? *Undoubtedly in prayer, more definite prayer, for missions.* It may be for the awakening of the mission spirit in the Church at large, or in his own church, or in special congregations. It may be for some special field. It may be, it must be, for himself very specially, that God would give and ever renew the mission fire from heaven. Whatever the prayer may be — the study must lead at once to more prayer, or the fruit will be comparatively small. Without prayer, even though there may be increased interest in missions, more work for them, better success in organization and greater finances, the real growth of the spiritual life and of the love of Christ in the people, may be very small.

When man's will and work are in the foreground, the spiritual life is weak; God's presence and power are little known. You may have people who read missionary books and faithfully give liberal contributions while there is little love to Christ or prayer for His kingdom. You may, on the other hand, have humble, simple people, who can give very little, but with that little they give their whole heart's love and prayer. The latter is on a higher and more spiritual level, in which the love of God is the supreme aim. No one needs to watch more carefully than the minister to see that the missionary enthusiasm he fosters in himself and others is, in very deed, the fire that comes from heaven in answer to believing prayer to consume the sacrifice. The missionary problem is a personal one. The minister who has solved it for himself will also be able to lead others to find its solution in the constraining power of Christ's love.

9

A Call to Prayer and Contrition

In the previous pages I have frequently spoken of prayer. As I come to the closing chapters of the book, I feel that all that has been said will profit little unless it leads to prayer. As we look at the extent of the field, and the greatness of the work that still has to be done; at the utterly inadequate force which the Church has at present on the field, we are crushed. We do not see sufficient signs that she is ready yet to place herself and all her resources at her Lord's disposal. We see our absolute impotence to give life either in the Church at home or the work abroad, and our entire dependence upon the power that comes from above in answer to prayer and faith. We are amazed at the love of our Lord to His people and to the perishing, and the promises He waits to fulfill. We feel that *our only hope is to apply ourselves to prayer*. Prayer, more prayer, much prayer, very special prayer, should first of all be made for the work to be done in our home churches on

147

behalf of foreign missions. That is indeed the one great need of the day. "Our help cometh from the Lord, who made heaven and earth."

I was somewhat surprised at the little direct mention at the Conference of prayer as one of the most important factors in mission work. Chapter VIII of the Report was indeed entitled *Prayer and Giving,* but almost all the addresses dealt chiefly with the latter. D. B. Eddy spoke of the unselfish prayer-life as developed by the use of prayer cycles. In her short but weighty address Mrs. J. H. Randall said:

> One great and imperative need of foreign misson work today is the almost forgotten secret of prevailing prayer. Missions have progressed so slowly abroad because piety and prayer have been so shallow at home. Get people *praying* for mission work, and they *must give.* Nothing but continuous prayer will solve the missionary problems of today. God must be petitioned to do these things for them. 'Ye have not because ye ask not.' God has promised great things to His Son and His Church concerning the unevangelized. God has promised great things to His children in the work of extending and hastening His kingdom. But notice — these promises are conditional. His Son, His Church, His Children, are *to intercede and to sacrifice.* The consequence of habitual intercession will be a new outpouring of the Holy Spirit upon the individual, the Church, and upon all the missionary work of the

world. Whoever prays most, helps most.

If these words are true — and they certainly are the very truth of God — surely the first concern of the leaders of mission work in our churches and societies, to whom the spiritual training of their members is entrusted by God should be to give prayer the same place in all their exhortations which it has in the purpose of God.

Rev. W. Perkins declared: The foreign mission movement was born in prayer, and prayer is the vital breath by which it lives. Great as the results are of foreign missions, *they would have been a hundredfold greater if the Church of Christ had been what she ought to be* in the two great matters of prayer and giving. What is needed is that the spiritual life of every Christian, and that of the whole Church, should be so deepened, instructed, and inspired by the Holy Ghost, that it shall become as natural and easy to pray daily for foreign missons as to pray for daily bread. The Church must develop the conviction that the law of sacrifice is the law of life, we must find time for prayer, even though it may mean withholding time from pleasure and business. Only sacrifice is fruitful.

There must be developed in the Church by the Spirit of God a penetrating and abiding sense of the world's urgent need, its misery, darkness and despair. A power must come that shall make the need so real, so terrible, that our first feeling shall be one of helplessness in the face of it; our next feeling, 'I must go and pray about it'; and the next, 'I will give up and sacrifice even necessities, in the presence of conditions like these for which Christ died.'

If these words are to be taken seriously and do any good, the great question is surely, how are the leaders of our mission work to awaken and to train the churches to that life of prayer of which they speak? If it be true, then the *results of foreign missions will be a hundredfold greater when the Church is what she ought to be in the matter of prayer.* Since there are many who give but do not pray, or give little and pray little, those who know what prayer is must pray and labor more earnestly. Let them pray that the life of Christians may be so deepened by the Holy Ghost, that it shall become "as natural and easy to pray daily for foreign missions as to pray for daily bread." God can do it. Let it be our definite aim and prayer — God *will* do it!

I trust that what I have said in regard to the place the Conference gave to the discussion of prayer will not be misunderstood. So much depends upon the law of proportion in the natural world. It is so in spiritual life, too. All evangelical teaching acknowledges the work of the Holy Spirit and the power of prayer to secure His working. There is no question that these truths have a place in the articles of our Creed. And yet it is only when they have *first place,* and everything else is made subordinate to them, that the Christian life will be truly healthy.

Of all the questions claiming the concern of the leaders of our mission work at home, there is not one that demands more urgent consideration, that is more difficult to decide, and that will bring a richer reward, than this: *How can the Churches be educated to more persistent, fervent, believing prayer?* Prayer will at once be the means and the proof of stronger Christian life, or more devotion to Christ's service, and of the blessing of heaven descending on our work. Much prayer would be the sign that we had found again the path by which the pentecostal Church entered on its triumphant course.

We cannot teach people to pray just by telling them to do so. Prayer is the pulse of the life. *The call to more prayer must be connected with the deepening of spiritual life.* The two great conditions of true prayer are an urgent sense of need, and a full assurance of a supply for that need. We must bring God's children to see and feel the need. The work entrusted to them; the obligation to do it; the consequence to ourselves, to Christ, to the perishing, of neglecting it; our absolute impotence to do it in our own strength — these great truths must master us. On the other side, the love of Christ to us and to the world; our access to God in Him as Intercessor; the certainty of persevering prayer being heard; the blessedness of a life of prayer; the blessings it can bring to the world — these, too, must grip us.

We must learn to pray in secret, to wait on God, to take hold of His strength. We must teach Christians to pray in little groups, with the joy and the love and the faith that fellowship brings. We must gather the whole

Church in special times of prayer, when His divine power will work above what we can ask or think.

In the heading of this chapter I have spoken of prayer and contrition. I somewhat missed this emphasis in the Conference. Incidental mention was frequently made about the shortcomings of pastors and laymen, in interest and prayer and giving, of the failure of the Church as a whole to do her duty. And yet where was the solemnity, the awesomeness of the neglect of our Lord's commission? Do we realize the terrible sin of disobedience of His last command, of the entire lack of sympathy with the desire for gratifying His love or seeking His glory? It was not emphasized as some think it should be, and must be, before a return to the true state of the Church can take place.

There is an optimism that loves to speak of what is bright and hopeful. It believes that in doing so thanks are brought to God and courage to His servants. Above everything it is afraid of pessimism. And yet optimism and pessimism are errors equally to be avoided. Each is one-sided; they are both extremes. Divine wisdom has taught us, "I lead (walk) in the midst of the paths of judgement." Experience teaches us that, when we have to deal with two apparently conflicting truths, there is only one way to see the true relation. We should look first to the one as if it were all, and thoroughly master all that it means. Then turn to the other, and grasp as fully all that it implies. When we know both, we are in a position to walk "in the midst" of the path of truth.

Apply this to missions. On the one side there is so much to rejoice in, to thank God for, and to take courage from. In the Conference report this note was often struck. Surely we never can give God too much praise for what He has done during the past century, and especially during the past twenty years. On the other hand, there is so much work that has not been done that could have been done, for the reason that the Church was not what she ought to be. Millions are perishing today without the knowledge of Christ, and will go on perishing, simply because the Church is not doing the work for which she was redeemed and endowed with God's Spirit. When we are brought face to face with this truth, our hearts will spontaneously cry out in contrition and shame. We will confess our sins. What sins? The sin of bloodguiltiness; the sin of disobedience; the sin of unbelief; the sin of selfishness and worldliness, grieving the Holy Spirit and quenching Christ's love in our hearts; the sin of not living wholly for Christ, for His love and His kingdom. These sins will become a burden greater than we can bear, until we have laid them at our Lord's feet and seen Him remove them.

These are not the sins of those who take no, or very little, interest in missions. In Scripture we find that the men who were most jealous for the honor of God, most diligent in His service, and least guilty of sin, were the first to confess it and mourn over it. Moses, David, Ezra, Nehemiah, and Daniel — the godliest men of their times — were the men most conscious of sin. Is not the sin of the vast majority of members to be counted as the sin of the whole body? I am speaking of the most devoted friends of Christ and of missions — the men who in church or society, as committee members or workers, are the leaders. These very men who, by virtue of their spiritual insight, ought to feel the sin most, to carry it to God, and then to appeal to the erring ones to come and join them in contrition and confession. We spoke of the need of a pentecostal era; it must be preceded by great repentance and turning from sin. This will not happen until the men, to whom the Lord gives the deepest sense of the sin of His people, have gathered them with a call to repentance and surrender to full obedience. The missionary appeal gives us one of the grandest opportunities for repentance as it uncovers the sins that lie at the root.

This has always been God's way: Contrition precedes restoration and renewal. On the day of Pentecost it was the preaching of "this same Jesus, *whom ye have crucified,*" that broke hearts, and prepared them for the receiving of the Holy Spirit. We still need the same kind of preaching to God's people. "This same Jesus," *whose command ye have disobeyed and neglected, whose love ye have despised and grieved,* "God hath made Him both Lord and Christ." If we are to summon Christians to a life of higher devotion in God's service, the wrong, the shame, the guilt of our present state must be set before them. It is when sin is felt and confessed, that Christ's pardoning love will be felt afresh. That new experience of His power and love will become the incentive to make that love known to others. It is the contrite heart that God makes alive. It is to the humbled soul that He gives more grace. An essential element in a true missionary revival will be a broken heart and a contrite spirit in view of past neglect and sin.

This preaching of contrition on account of our lack of obedience to Christ's great command will be no easy thing. It will need men who wait before God for the vision of what this sin of the Church really implies.

Hudson Taylor spent five years in China feeling its darkness without grasping its full significance. He spent five more years in England working and praying for China; he still did not know how great its awful need was. Only when he began to prepare a statement for publication on China's needs did he feel the full horror of the thick darkness. He could find no rest until God gave him the twenty-four workers he had prayed for, and he was willing to accept the responsibility to lead them out. We shall require men who give themselves, in study and prayer and love, to take in all the terrible meaning of the words we utter so easily — that the Church is disobedient to her Lord's last and greatest command.

In such contrition the pastors must take the lead. The preaching of contrition cannot be in power if the pastor has no experience of it. The missionary problem is a personal one — to the pastor, too. Both on his own behalf and as representative of the people, he must take the lead. "Let the priests, the ministers of the Lord, weep between the porch and the altar and say, Spare Thy people, O Lord, and give not Thine heritage to reproach, that the heathen should rule over them." (Joel 2:17) Is there any one church or parish of which it can in truth be said that the extension of Christ's kingdom is the one goal for which it lives? Do not all admit that the Church is not what she should be? And is it not plain that if this continues, the evangelization of the world in this generation will be impossible?

With the Church as a whole so guilty before God, should not every minister take some part of the blame for this condition? Should he not seek with his people to come under the deep conviction that they have not given themselves to Christ with entire devotion; that they have not sufficiently renounced their own interests and ease, and the spirit of the world, to carry out His great command with all their strength? And why? Because their heart and life have not been wholly yielded to the transforming power of Christ's spirit and love.

Although we all in some degree share this responsibility, there is no possible way for the ministry to remove the evil and promote a better state, without every one of us confessing our lack of that enthusiastic love to Christ which would have enabled us to be true witnesses to Him. When the spirit of contrition takes hold of the ministry, there will be hope for the people. If in public preaching and praying the tone of contrition and confession is clear and deep, there will surely be a response in the hearts of all earnest people. Those who are now our best contributors will feel how much more God asks — and is willing to give, through His Holy Spirit — of fervent love and prevailing prayer, and full consecration of all to His service. It will be proved in our mission work: "He that humbleth himself shall be exalted." Repentance is always the gate to larger blessing.

What did He who holds the seven stars in His right hand say to the Church of Ephesus? "I know thy works, and thy labor, and thy patience, and how thou canst not bear them that are evil; and thou has tried them which say they are apostles, and are not, and hast found them liars: and hast borne, and hast patience, and for My Name's sake has labored, and hast not fainted." This certainly seemed to be a model church. What diligence and zeal in good works; what patience in suffering; what purity in discipline; what zeal for orthodoxy; and what unwearied perseverance in it all! And best of all, it was for His Name's sake. And yet the Lord was not satisfied. "Nevertheless I have somewhat against thee, because *thou hast left thy first love. Remember therefore from whence thou art fallen, and repent,* and do the first works; or else I will come unto thee quickly, and remove thy candlestick out of her place, *except thou repent."*

The Church had lost her first love. The tenderness and fervor of the personal attachment to the Lord Jesus was now lacking. The works were still being done in His Name but they were no longer like the first works, in the spirit of their first love. He calls them to contrition, to look back, and repent, and do the first works. It is possible to work much and earnestly for Christ and His cause in commendable ways as far as man can judge; but there may be lacking that without which the works are *as nothing* in His sight. He counts love the greatest of all — the love of a personal attachment to Christ. God is Love. Christ loved us and gave Himself. His love was a tender, holy giving of Himself, a personal friendship and fellowship. That love of His, cherished in the heart in daily close communion, responded to by a love that clings to Him, proved by His love pervading all our labor for others — *it is that which makes our work acceptable.* It was this first love to Christ which gave the pentecostal Church its power. It was this pentecostal love which Christ calls them to remember, from which they were fallen, and to which, in repentance, they were to return. Nothing less can satisfy the heart of Him who loved us. Shall we not give it to Him?

It is this pentecostal love to which we must return in our mission work. We saw how God made the Moravian church the first church of the Reformation to take the pentecostal stand, and give herself wholly to bringing the gospel to every creature. We saw that it was love — a passionate, adoring contemplation of Christ's dying love, a passionate desire to make that love known. That was the key. *Missions was the automatic outflow and overflow of their love for Christ.* It was to satisfy Christ's love and express their own love that they brought to Him souls that He had died to save. That made the most insignificant of churches the greatest of all. As we mourn over the state of the Church, with all its unfaithfulness to Christ and to the perishing souls of the unevangelized, let us, above all, make confession of the loss of our first love. Remember how even Peter, after his fall from his first love, could not be restored till the searching question, *"Lovest thou Me?"* had deeply wounded him. Then he penitently, but confidently, answered, "Thou knowest that *I love Thee."*

And as we repent and mourn the past, let us press on to wait before our Lord with the one prayer:

Love, Lord! it is Thy love we need. We know about it; we have preached it; we have sought to find it. But now we wait in humility and reverance and wonder before Thee. O Loving One, shed that love abroad in our hearts by Thy Holy Spirit. We look to Thee to enable us in the power of that love to take the world into our hearts. Like Thee, we want to live and die only that Thy love may triumph over every human soul!

To implement the principles set forth in *The Key to the Missionary Problem,* Andrew Murray gave a special message to pastors and recommended a week of prayer. We have included both for your consideration. Although his recommendations were primarily directed to the circumstances of his generation, many are valid for today.

Every minister holds office under the great commission. Therefore, each of us should take to heart the entire world-wide field. In addition to the corner committed to our care, we are responsible for aiding in getting the whole occupied. Each of us needs to study our Commission afresh, to see that we rightly understand and truly fulfill it. Let us, in view of the sad failure of the Church, and the cry for the restoration of the pentecostal state, once again listen to the words in which our Lord entrusts us with the commission to see that His love reaches every human being.

"AND JESUS SAID, *ALL POWER* IS GIVEN UNTO ME IN HEAVEN AND IN EARTH"

The ALL of unlimited power

Jesus reveals Himself as the Omnipotent One, seated at God's right hand, ruling in the midst of His enemies, making His people willing in the day of His power. That was His Coronation day, when He received the Spirit to fill His disciples with power, and make thousands, even of those who had crucified Him, bow at His feet

In this Jesus, the Triumphant Lord, missions have their origin, their power, their certainty of success. The word He spoke made His disciples strong. Let us humbly bow and wait until the vision and the word of the Omnipotent Christ deliver us from every fear, whether of the Church's not being willing in the day of His power, or of His enemies not bowing at His feet.

"GO YE THEREFORE, TEACH *ALL NATIONS,* AND PREACH THE GOSPEL TO *EVERY CREATURE"*
The ALL of unbounded love

He died for all; His dying love thirsted for all; His love in heaven seeks all. In these words "all nations" and "every creature" He reveals to His Church the boundless love that is to be the measure of their love. In these words He speaks into the very heart of His people, and there begins to burn within them a love that cannot rest till every living being knows of Jesus.

Brother ministers! Has this love got possession? Does it burn in us?

"TEACHING THEM TO OBSERVE *ALL THINGS* WHATSOEVER I HAVE COMMANDED YOU"
The ALL of universal obedience

He had taught His disciples the heavenly blessedness of obedience. "If ye love Me, keep My commandments: and the Father will send you the Spirit; and the Father will love you; and I will love you; and I will manifest Myself to you; and We will come and make Our abode with you; and ye shall abide in My love; and ye shall be My friends" (John 14:15). They were to go out, that the vilest and most hardened, His very enemies and murderers, might be changed and be taught to observe all things whatsoever He had commanded.

Brother ministers! Have we understood the high aim of our commission — to lead to a life of personal obedience to Him, and teach the Church universal obedience?

"AND LO, I AM WITH YOU *ALL THE DAYS,* EVEN UNTO THE END OF THE WORLD"

The ALL of unceasing fellowship

The commission ends where it began — with Jesus Himself. First it was His Power; here it is His Presence. All the days, and all the day, His Divine abiding fellowship is to be the portion of His obedient disciple. No trials or difficulties, however dark; no labors, however wearying or fruitless; no opposition or suffering, however painful; no conscious weakness or unworthiness, however great, can break this promise. Nothing can prevent His holy, blessed fellowship with His servant. To every one who accepts the Commission and lives under it, the holy nearness of Jesus is secured.

Brother ministers! Let us seek by the Holy Spirit a deeper, a fuller entrance into our Lord's commission, and an entire surrender to His service: He will make His promise true.

Common men do uncommon tasks

What was it that enabled poor fishermen and common men so simply to accept, and so loyally to carry out, such a divine commission? Two things.

The one was: *Their hearts had been prepared for it by their intense devotion to Jesus.* They had learned to love Him. They had gone down with Him into His death. They had been quickened in His resurrection life. He was their all in all. His words were to them as water to the thirsty.

The other: *It was Jesus Himself who spoke the words.* Not a book or a messenger, but Jesus Himself. Oh! come, let us rise from looking at the commission to look at our

Ascended Lord, and wait on Him. Let us patiently bow for Him to reveal first the Power in which He works. Then will we feel the Love with which He longs for every man. Our obedience will lead us to the joy of His unchanging Presence. We too, as the most ordinary disciples did, must learn to wait to be clothed with power, so that in part we may help in leading Christ's Church back to its pentecostal fulness of the Spirit for the work it has to do.

PROPOSAL — A WEEK OF PRAYER

The question has come to me very strongly whether it would be possible, in view of all that was said at the Conference of the shortcomings of the leadership and the membership, to gather God's people for specific and united prayer. We would consider the greatness of the work to be done, the call to confession and repentance, and the need of an entirely new standard of devotion throughout the Church. We would enjoy the certainty that in answer to prayer God will open the windows of heaven and pour out His blessing.

The Conference was indeed representative of the whole Church; but I am afraid that only a very small fraction of the Church members will become acquainted with what was said, or profit by its instruction. The expression was used, *"If this Conference and those whom it represents will do their duty . . ."* Why not bring our representatives into contact with their large constituency, so that all might be awakened and renewed?

My first thought was whether some of the Committee, who had so enthusiastically labored for the mission cause in the Conference, could not devise some scheme by which the many earnest appeals might be shared with all the churches. But I realize there would be difficulties. To be effective, it would almost need a new organization with a large machinery.

But then I was reminded of a world-wide organization, with all its machinery ready. We have the

the Evangelical Alliance, and the already set up Week of Prayer in the first week of each January. It would be something wonderful and blessed if the whole Church would gather at her Lord's feet for a whole week and devote herself to *prayer specifically for the extension of the kingdom through missions.* There could be no grander opportunity for instruction as to the will of God and His promises; the greatness of the work and its urgency; the claim of Christ on the world and every creature in it as His inheritance, and on His people to be the willing messengers of His love. It would be an ideal occasion to enforce Christ's last command and rouse the children of God to prayer and consecration.

Would it not bring health and blessing to many if the Church would unite in presenting herself before God with the one prayer that all who have sinned through ignorance or weakness may be roused to begin the work that is waiting for them? Such an awakening of true mission interest would be a beginning of the quickening of spiritual life, and might greatly strengthen the desire for that renewal in larger measure. But how to get the churches to act together, and the church members to gather before God for instruction and prayer? We can hardly conceive of a more glorious opportunity than a Week of Prayer would afford.

Would not our missionaries on the fields welcome such a proposal and be greatly strengthened by its result? They would feel inspired that the whole Church was giving a week to spend with them before the throne of their Lord, in order to receive new instruction and equipment from God for work. It would be an invaluable lesson to the new-born churches on the fields that the life we offer them is a life from above, to be received and dispensed only in answer to prayer. They and we would feel how truly we are "one new man in Christ Jesus." And God, our God, would bless us!

The new twentieth century calls us to intensified prayer. Much has been said of the past having been a missionary center. We thank God for all that He has accomplished in it through His people. But all admit that *unless the Church begins to live and love, to give and pray, on a very different scale from what she has been doing, there is not the least prospect of the evangelization of the world within this generation.* The first year of the new century is passing. We have had time to consider whether there are any signs of change in our devotion. We have had the opportunity of calculating what is needed if the work is to be done. How could we consecrate the century more effectually to God than by beginning its second year with a grand muster of the whole army of God on earth to renew its vow: *The whole earth for Christ Jesus; His gospel for every creature?*

At this point Andrew Murray offered varied recommendations as to what the churches of his day might do to prepare for and carry out such a Week of Prayer. Different churches and societies could, as far as possible, cooperate in united prayer meetings. If such meetings were not practical, men of missionary enthusiasm or of spiritual power might travel among various churches. Gain for any specific mission board would not be the paramount motivation for this week; sharing of blessings received from God and praying for the whole world's needs and workers would take the priority.

Special studies of the missionary question could be sponsored in local churches. There might be the preaching of a series of missionary sermons before the Week of Prayer. Evangelists might be asked to give up their ordinary preaching of salvation messages for one week in order to extend their help in this combined effort of winning the world for Christ.

Preparation by special literature was considered highly strategic because many Christians were uninformed about the basic facts of foreign missions, even the Biblical basis and the spirit of the great commission. He recommended the writing of a number of simple, pointed leaflets and booklets to this end. Further, that four to six men of spiritual power might each write a paper on some different aspect of the great missions question, which could be issued as pamphlets.

As to the logistics of the labor connected with the preparation and execution of such a Week of Prayer, he suggested that a number of known leaders in mission work might be invited or appointed as a Committee of Management. Certain men among them could be set apart by this body to circulate information, awaken interest, secure cooperation, and enlist local helpers.

The Student Volunteer Movement was fruitfully active in missions in those days, particularly in training those who were ready to go to the foreign field. Murray suggested that they might offer themselves to pastors to help in meetings for creating missionary interest. Especially might this be an advantage because of the difficulty of securing a visit from a missionary for every congregation. Murray continued, "A missionary candidate, full of enthusiasm, who has studied some part of the mission field, or better, a team of two or three, testifying to what their Lord has done for them, and their surrender to His service, might in many cases supply the lack. This would result in a returned blessing to themselves as well as to the churches."

Extraordinary circumstances require extraordinary measures. The discovery of an imminent danger justifies exceptional changes, and men willingly approve and submit to the inconvenience. The state of the Church, the need of the world, the command of Christ, appear to me to call for very special efforts. The urgency of the case is extreme. We should not lose time. Our Master wishes every human being without delay to know of His having come to the world to save him.

Let not the enthusiasm of our slogan, *In this generation!* deceive us. It may tend to make us satisfied to let the millions a year pass away in darkness without knowing Him. We may be deceived with the idea that it eventually is going to be done before this generation ends. But it most certainly is *not going to be done* if the Church remains at her present level.

The task is so large, it is so difficult, it needs such an interposition of divine power, that, unless the Church returns to the pentecostal life of her first love, it cannot and will not be done. I say again, the urgency of the case is extreme. No sacrifice can be too great if we can only get the Church, or the more earnest part of it, to take time and wait unitedly before the Throne of God, to review her position and to confess her shortcomings. Then she can go forward to claim God's promise of power, and to consecrate her all to His service. I think that devoting a week exclusively to foreign missions would be pleasing to God and acceptable to His people, and bring abundant blessing.

We would gather as one great company throughout the world to ask the Master to repeat to us the great commission, and breathe its power into our hearts. As our hearts would open up in faith to the promise of His infinite power and unchanging presence with us; as we would yield ourselves in fresh obedience and consecration to the work of His love, His blessing and His Spirit would surely be given us.

I believe that many who have been laboring heartily in this blessed service will be brought near their blessed Lord, and fired with new zeal to lead on others who are lagging behind. Many who have been giving something, and praying or loving a little, will be taught to see the true secret of partnership with Christ in this work. Many will hear a call to consider whether the Lord wants their personal service in the field. Many a pastor will get new insight into what he really has to train his people for. He will see too, how much, even while laboring at home, he may do for the world at large. I am confident that to many it may be made the exciting beginning of a new revelation of what our Lord Jesus is and claims. We will experience the inexpressible blessedness of, like our Lord, living only to bring the world back to God.

I leave the proposal in the hands of those who have the power to decide. Should there be good reasons for not going forward with this recommendation of setting aside the general curriculum of prayer during that annual week to concentrate on prayer for missions, I shall not regret having made the proposal. It may be used to direct attention to a great need, and in God's good time bring forth fruit in a way we do not expect. I commit the thought to His gracious care.

And may the day speedily come when His Church shall, in waiting on God, renew her youth and her strength; when the glory of the Lord shall be revealed, and all flesh shall see it together.

SUGGESTIONS FOR A WEEK OF PRAYER
FOR FOREIGN MISSIONS

FIRST DAY
PRAISE Psalm 145:11-13

Praise God. For the glory of His kingdom in the earth; — for what He has accomplished; for the share He gives us in His work; for what He is doing and is going to do. 2 Chron. 20:14-22.

SECOND DAY.
THE WORK AND THE WORKERS

The Work. Its extent. (Statistics of the unevangelized) 2 Cor. 2:16 Its difficulty. The power of Satan. Eph. 6:12 Its urgency. The worth of one soul; millions a year dying.

The Workers. The Church, the Body of Christ. Every member, without exception, redeemed to take part in that work. Phil. 2:15, 16.

Pray. For a vision of the need of the world, of the glory of Christ, of the calling of believers; for all missionaries, our representatives in the field. Col. 4:2-4.

THIRD DAY.
THE POWER FOR THE WORK —
THE HOLY SPIRIT

The Holy Spirit. All mission work is God's own work. 1 Cor. 12:6. The Holy Spirit is the Mighty Power of God working in us. Eph. 3:16, 17, 20. The Spirit given at Pentecost as the power to bring the gospel to every person. John 15:26, 27; Acts 1:8. All failure owing to the loss of this power. Gal. 3:3. All genuine mission work, in giving, praying, working, only of value if the power of the Spirit is in it. Rom. 15:16. God's promise of the Spirit meeting us, and our prayer for the Spirit meeting us, the only hope for our missions. Acts 4:31.

Pray. For the power of the Spirit as the enthusiasm of Christ's presence and love in the Church, in missionary societies, in your own congregation, in your own life, with the one aim of witnessing of Jesus to every human soul. Luke 24:47; Acts 1:8.

FOURTH DAY.
CONTRITION AND CONFESSION

Confession. Of the terrible failure of the Church to know and fulfill her mission. Of the lack of entire consecration to Christ's honor and kingdom. Of the lack of love and self-sacrifice in giving and praying. Hag. 1:11; Mal. 3:10; Phil. 2:21.

Contrition. Repentance, the only path to restoration. Isa. 58:1, 2, 6, 7; Gen. 42:21. Pray for the Spirit to convince of sin.

FIFTH DAY.
THE SPIRIT OF SUPPLICATION

Prayer. Its place. The chief factor on man's side in doing God's work. The key to all heavenly blessing and power. Luke 11:13; John 14:13, 14; Eph. 3:20.

Its difficulty. It needs the crucifixion of the flesh to strive and labor (agonize) Rom. 15:30; Col. 4:12, to watch in prayer. It needs a spiritual mind to delight in fellowship with Christ, and to believe that our prayers will prevail.

Its urgent necessity. More men and more money are needed; but the need of more prayer is greater, such as ushered in Pentecost. Acts 1:14.

Pray. That in this week of prayer God may give us the spirit of prayer; that there may be a great increase of secret, habitual, fervent, believing intercession for the power of the Spirit in our mission work.

SIXTH DAY.
CONSECRATION AND SERVICE

Consecration. If confession has been real, if prayer has been honest, there must follow a new surrender. 2 Chron. 15:8-15. This implies a turning away from all sin and from all shortcoming to a life of entire obedience and devotion. 2 Cor. 5:15.

It implies especially a very personal giving of one's self to the Lord Jesus and His love, to be kept by Him and used, as His own property and possession. 2 Tim. 2:21; Tit. 2:14. Everything depends on this: the missionary problem is a personal one.

Service. It implies that we serve Christ by seeking souls for Him. Isa. 53:10. In concern for missions by interest, and giving, and praying, and fellowship with others. And also in making Him known to those around us.

SEVENTH DAY.
FAITH AND ITS DIVINE POSSIBILITIES

Faith. The power in man that corresponds to the power of God. Matt. 19:26; Mark 9:23. It is the power that leads to prayer, grows strong in prayer, and prevails in prayer. Mark 11:24. It is the power that overcomes the world, because Christ has overcome it, and faith lives in union with Him. John 16:33; I John 5:4, 5.

Missions have no foundation or law but in God's purpose, God's promise, God's power. These Divine possibilities are the food of faith. and call every mission friend to this one thing — to be strong in faith, giving glory to God. Rom. 4:20, 21.

Pray. That this week may lead to a deep revelation of God's readiness and power to fulfill His promises to His people, and a great quickening of true faith in every mission worker and helper at home and abroad.

FINAL DAY.
THE LOVE OF CHRIST. ROM. 8:31

Its triumph in every human heart our aim. Phil. 2:13. Its possession our only power for living and witnessing. 2 Cor. 5:14. Let us once more saturate our spirits with the Moravian motivation to missions:

"Get this burning thought of **personal love for the Saviour who redeemed me** into the hearts of all Christians, and you have the **most powerful incentive for missionary effort** of every kind.

"Oh! if we could make this problem a personal one, if we could fill the hearts of the people with a personal love for the Saviour who died for them, **the indifference of Christendom would disappear, and the kingdom of Christ would appear!"**